REPLACE YOURSELF

REPLACE YOURSELF

YOURSELF

THE TECH GEEK'S GUIDE TO
NAVIGATING LEADERSHIP

ROB LA GESSE

REPLACE YOURSELF

The Tech Geek's Guide to Navigating Leadership

ISBN   978-1-5445-0343-1 *Paperback*

978-1-5445-0342-4 *Ebook*

I want to thank my now-adult children, Derek and Lauren. Not because they directly helped me with the book, but because they gave me the greatest gift a father could ever receive—unconditional love and support—even when shit got squirrely as we navigated custody issues, moved from state to state, dealt with too many hurricanes, and just figured each other out as we got older, and I got older still.

I am so proud of them and thankful for them.

CONTENTS

INTRODUCTION

People don't like my ideas. At least, not at first.

When I moved into the communications and PR division of Rackspace, I wanted to build a social media presence that differed from most, if not all, other public companies. Most of them were run by marketing agencies, organizations designed to push content on customers. Instead, I wanted to have a conversation with our customers, particularly when they engaged our social accounts to complain about a problem.

With a marketing team in charge, the response to a customer issue was always the same: "Please contact our support team at blah blah blah."

As you can imagine, that response left customers even more upset than they were when they decided to comment on our social media pages. Chances were they'd already contacted customer support and gotten nowhere.

I needed a team that could be more proactive. More hands on. People who had the credentials to log in to the support systems and directly address the customers' needs; who had the tools, the knowledge, and the internal contacts to get shit done.

I needed engineers.

ENGINEERS DON'T DO CUSTOMER SUPPORT

Like I said, people don't always like my ideas. The people who ran the customer support side of the company were no different. Some thought I was usurping their control, streamlining the process, or worse yet, they feared I was creating a new support channel, one that bypassed their ticketing system by sending customers straight to our social media account. My team and I were seen as butting in where we didn't belong.

The problem with all of that was simple: it worked.

We didn't undermine or cannibalize our support teams. We created an escalation path instead of a replacement path. If a customer utilized social media to lodge a complaint without a ticket number, we rerouted them to the proper support channel, where they would follow the normal process. Because my team of engineers had the skillset to address a large number of complaints directly, we could access the information from that ticket number and immediately address the next steps and solve the issue.

Our customer satisfaction rates increased considerably as a result. If a customer had an issue and an unresolved ticket number at eight o'clock at night with eight hours gone and no resolution, our team didn't have to redirect them.

In doing so, we earned a reputation for using social media as a customer service vehicle. We were one of the first large companies ever to do so, and people took notice. I did a number of talks at both marketing and customer support conventions about our methodology. Large companies like USAA and AT&T called on our team to work with theirs on how to use social media for customer satisfaction and not just for marketing.

BUT...ENGINEERS?

Yes, engineers. Look, I get it. If you're in an industry where you work with engineers, developers, or anyone in the technical professions, I'd venture those individuals are the last people who come to your mind when it comes to customer support. In fact, I'd go so far as to say that you don't imagine there's much else they would do besides code and develop software—isolated in a cubicle, earbuds in, closed off from the rest of the world.

If you can't see them in marketing or support, you certainly don't guess they'd be a fit for leadership. In fact, they themselves might not guess it either.

You'd both guess wrong.

I know because I made that transition, and I'm going to tell you how.

First, understand that while I transcended my role as an engineer and software developer into the management realms of marketing and PR, I don't claim to be an expert in either. In fact, for the purposes of this book, I don't need to be. What *is* important is that I was extremely successful in both worlds and that I learned an immense amount from being immersed in those two very disparate settings. This allowed me to become something crucial for you.

An interpreter.

THE GEEK'S DILEMMA

As a tech geek, one who is especially good at your job, chances are you don't yet have the inner (or outer) voice that gives you the confidence to move above your current station. You don't feel you have the ability or the tools to best communicate with other departments like sales and marketing.

You're probably right.

It's through no fault of your own. It's due in large part to the way we think about engineers in this day and age: we think of the guy or gal in a dark room coding all day, solitary, headphones on all the time. Nobody wanting to interrupt them because everyone is saying that what they are doing is critically important.

Much of this perception of what you do and who you are stems from the ways you've been trained and the ways in which your skills are utilized. The problem with that is you condition yourself to believe these things about yourself that everyone else does. That's fine until someone from management comes into your dark little room, turns on the lights, puts a name tag on your door, and tells you that you've been moved into management.

It's terrifying for so many reasons. You feel a ton of pressure when you're offered a promotion. You think, *Shit, they want to promote me and if I don't take it, I'm not going to be seen as a team player. What if I don't take it, and one of my coworkers becomes my boss? If I reject the offer, does this mean I'll never get another raise?* You're also faced with the idea of no longer being a daily contributor to the technical aspects of your job, the thing you were trained to do best.

Those ideas, though? They're in your head. Internally placed. None of those worries are actually true unless you make them so.

Understand that if you're a good developer or engineer, your company knows this, and they still think that a better place for you is in leadership, managing other developers. They are taking a known quantity out of a productive position because they are hoping to invest in you to expand and spread your knowledge, grow your contribution, and increase the overall productivity of the company by promoting you.

I've personally witnessed the need for engineers to become leaders quickly and watched their high rate of failure. I've watched companies lose a strong developer and gain a weak leader. I wanted to write a book that leverages my experience, mistakes, and successes in a language that technical professionals will understand.

I did. You're reading it now.

YOU *CAN* DO THIS

There are not many engineers writing new code these days. More often than not, when you're writing code and you don't know how to do something, you'll do a Google search to find a snip of the code, adjust it for your needs, and use it. You learn to create and write code from those examples.

In this book, I'll give you examples from my own personal experience with this journey to tell you how you'll learn to go from the person who makes the widget to the person who decides to order more widgets. You won't use them all. You'll take snips from this one experience, pieces from another one, and come out better prepared for a move into management on the other side faster than you thought possible.

Most developers work on projects they have to deliver this week, next week, or in a month. Management means looking at the long game and knowing how to "see around corners" to anticipate problems before they occur. Based on real-life encounters and experiences, you'll learn what it takes to go from a development mindset to a management one.

Perhaps most important of all, you'll learn how to prevent the washout cycle. Too many times in my career, I've seen good developers who had the potential to be great managers fail once promoted and return to their original position, or worse, leave the company or get fired. It happened because they had no one who spoke their language to prepare them for what was to come.

I speak your language. I understand how the engineering mind works. Trust me to guide you along the path so you only have to do this once. There will be no restarts. This book will explain the journey in a manner that resonates with your technical mindset and will prepare you for a career of continued success.

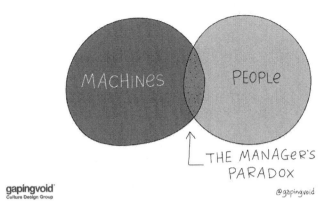

MACHINES PEOPLE

↳ THE MANAGER'S PARADOX

THIS IS NO DIET BOOK

Know that there are no recipes contained within. Nowhere will I tell you to prepare your food in exactly this manner, eat exactly on this schedule every month, and you'll end up with washboard abs.

There is no formula for success for you to follow, no playbook that tells you how to get it all right because, quite simply, everyone is different. Each person reading this book will take something different from the experiences I share. Some chapters might not even apply to you, and that's okay. Just like taking those snips of code to create a new set of code, use the stories and lessons provided here to assist you where you feel you need it the most.

This is also not a guide about how to get promoted. The

truth is, if you're reading this, you should already be on that path.

This is a book about how to *deal* with getting promoted and how to be successful once it occurs. It is a source of reference—a series of situational examples on which you can look back when you encounter similar challenges to mine. It's about how to reframe your thinking such that you retain the ability to maintain contact with your community of developers and engineers but also become cognizant of the larger realities of the company that you're now being paid to address.

You're not just being paid to deliver a widget anymore. You're getting paid to figure out what new widget is coming out next year or how many the company will need to supply the demand. That's a different type and level of thinking, one you're not used to and one of which you think you're not capable.

You're wrong, and I'll show you how.

YOU WILL FUCK UP

If I had to read a book by some guy telling me about all the wonderful things he'd done over a storied career where he'd made absolutely no mistakes—well, I wouldn't put myself in a situation where I had to read that book because I would *not* read that book.

The truth is that people, especially high achievers, are afraid to share their failures—that is, if they'll admit they've had them at all.

You are going to fail in your journey. It's how you frame those failures—seeing them as opportunities for improvement—that will determine how you let those failures affect your trajectory. It's not enough, however, for me to just tell you that it's okay for you to fail and to embrace it.

Instead of beginning this path with some epic success, let's take a look at how I fucked up royally, and how it was one of the best things I could have done.

CHAPTER ONE

SHARE MISTAKES

When I was the director of software development, I did not get involved in the technical analysis of potential job candidates. I was focused on fit and finish. I expected my teams to do all of the technical vetting, and then I would come in at the end to see not only if the candidate was a good fit for the team but if the team was a good fit for them.

I had a highly respected employee, someone in whom I had a lot of trust, particularly in his technical ability and skillset. He was incredibly productive—always met his deliverables, always with high quality. After a series of interviews, he gave his sign-off on one particular individual, so we moved him on in the hiring process.

You can tell a lot about a person when you put them in certain social settings. I like to take them to a restaurant.

The way someone treats the waitstaff can tell you a lot about the type of person they are.

This guy treated them like shit.

Team dynamics are so critical to success, and watching this candidate in the restaurant gave me a bad feeling in my gut that hiring him would be a bad move. However, the technical accolades were so high from the other team members with whom he'd interviewed, especially from the team lead I so immensely trusted, that I ignored my instincts and went with their recommendation.

We hired him. He left within three months.

The recruiter's time; the cost of advertising the position; the time it took to interview the ten other candidates; our phone interviews with the recruiter; flying the candidate out and paying for his hotel, meals, and transportation; the candidate spending five hours at the company meeting with the different teams—it all added up to a tab of over $50,000.

There is a hidden cost of business to which people do not pay attention. All of those teams involved in the interview process had to be pulled from their daily tasks, which means they were not producing during that time. There is also the additional cost of relocating candidates if they don't live locally.

Not to mention that engineers don't want to be interviewing candidates. They would almost rather go rewrite code they wrote a year ago, and we both know there are few things an engineer dislikes more than rework. Bringing on an employee who doesn't work out in a matter of three months means you're starting over from scratch. Not only are you subjecting your company to the expense, but you're putting your team through something they'd rather not do.

Of course, it sucks for the candidate too. I'm not saying that as a leader you should, on a whim because of a gut feeling, decide not to hire someone. At the same time, you have those instincts for a reason. Talk about them so you can make the most informed decision for your company and your team.

My mistake was I let my engineering brain override my instinct because other engineers told me how brilliant this guy was, how good he was at coding, and how successful he'd been in his career. I let all that outweigh the notion that his successes as an individual cannot be more important than his ability to work within a team. If someone is not a fit, they become a pariah, giving them even less of a chance at success because they don't get invited to the meetings, the get-togethers, or the parties. They get cut off because no one wants them in the room.

We had a saying at Rackspace that we didn't hire brilliant

assholes. It wasn't written into our core philosophy. You wouldn't see it hanging on a plaque as part of our mission statement. Still, almost everyone in the company knew it and talked about it.

I broke that core tenet and paid for it, figuratively and quite literally. During the period when this candidate was failing, we had a bad financial quarter. As a result, we paused hiring. When it came time to let him go, I could not replace him. I no longer had the headcount or the budget to do that. This was also significant as the plan was to bring in the new hire to elevate the team, which would have meant promoting the hiring manager, which would have more easily allowed for the planned transition into another department for me.

DON'T BOUNCE BAD APPLES

One of the core values of Rackspace is friends and family. When I was there, we tried to treat everyone as though they were just that.

The truth is that some people take that too fucking far.

They allow it to affect their decision-making, particularly when it comes to firing someone. They think, *we don't fire our friends. We don't fire our brother-in-law.* That simply cannot be true, particularly in a public company. If your friends or your brother-in-law aren't doing their jobs, then they need to go. What they don't need to do is be transferred to another department across the hall where they're going to become somebody else's problem.

I call it bouncing bad apples. It's a terrible practice, but it's one people engage in when they don't want to admit they've made a mistake. I've seen it in a number of companies, both public and private. I've watched bad apples bounced around for years before someone finally steps up to fire them. Sometimes I've had to be that person. More than once, I've gotten pushback from the person who hired them that the individual worked for them and they were great.

Oh, really? Then why did you move them out of your department after just four months?

Invariably the answer is almost always, "He just didn't fit my team." I shit you not, I've heard that about one person from five teams. Not at five different companies. One apple got bounced to five different teams. What would possibly make me rationalize that number six was going to be the charm?

The problem with apple bouncing is you imbue these people with a sense of entitlement. They get a sense of arrogance that makes them feel like they're part of the "good old boys" network. They think, *I've been here longer than half of you.* If I miss my meetings or don't hit my quotas? Whatever. We don't fire good old boys.

I'll fire good old boys, and I'll do it quickly. Quicker yet, I'll promote the people who need promoting—the people who deserve it.

Bouncing bad apples is a prime example of not owning your mistakes. If you make a bad hire, the easiest thing for you to do is to pull that employee aside and tell them they should start looking for someplace to move within the company. It's the easy thing for you as a leader because you don't have to write anything down. You don't have to submit anything to human resources. You don't have to put the employee on an improvement plan nor do you have to manage that plan.

All you do is give them a little head-nod warning to find something else. When they interview with another team, the team leader goes to HR to inquire on the status of that employee, and what do they see? Nothing negative. All good. Feel free to move them over.

You screwed over another team because you were a coward. You were intellectually lazy, and you were emotionally unable to make the decisions you were paid to make—the tough calls. If you move a bad apple to another bush, you're going to end up with another bush of bad apples. Do the right thing.

Send them to your competitor.

I'm not joking. As the director of a previous company, I kept a stack of our competitors' business cards on my desk. When I had an employee that I knew wasn't going to work out, I'd hand them the competitor's card and tell them to use it because it just wasn't going to work out with us.

MANAGE GROWTH, NOT YOUR SLICE OF THE PIE

Your job as a leader is not to just focus on your team winning but the wins of the company as a whole.

This means you don't just focus your efforts on whether or not your team has the best coffee in their break room, or making sure they have the nicest chairs, or that they all get a new computer every year.

That's what a team leader does. That is not what managers, directors, or above do.

Directors and above have to manage the pie, not the slices. How do the decisions that you make for your team help grow the whole pie for the entire company, not just your slice? If the pie grows, everyone eats. Rising tides and all that.

The problems arise when people assume leadership positions and invest all of their efforts into growing their team. Before you know it, the team has grown so large that it surpasses critical mass and now contains dead weight—apples that need to be tossed. The team has sixty people when it used to have twenty. Business needs change, and now you have forty people you no longer need—people you will now need to lay off because you managed your team and not the interests of the company.

Business directions change all the time, and you have to build and manage your teams with that knowledge in mind. Sometimes that means making hard decisions about who needs to stay and who needs to go when the needs of the company calls for it. Unfortunately, it's not always bad apples. Business moves at light speed, and if you are focused on what you built yesterday, you're going to lose it unless you are modifying it for what you need tomorrow.

A good leader has to constantly reevaluate their own teams, even if it's a good team. Sometimes that means making the tough call to let good people go.

You have to own your mistakes. More importantly, you

can't make your mistakes someone else's problem. If you do this, you'll be amazed at what can happen. I'm friends with almost every employee I've had to lay off simply because I owned it. It took a long time for some of them to come around, but when they reached out, they told me they realized it wasn't about them. It was about business. Some even said that since it happened, they'd never been happier.

KICK IN YOUR GEEK BRAIN

As a technical person, so much of this likely sounds foreign to you.

The truth is that once you are promoted to a position of leadership, you are now a people person whether you like it or not. When you're sitting in your cubicle with your earbuds on in the dark, you are not a people person—you are an individual contributor. As soon as you have somebody working for you, you become a people person. Once you assume that role, emotions and relationships matter. A lot. If you end up the type of leader I am and like many other leaders I know, you'll end up friends with a good number of your employees.

That's when you'll need to rely on the analytical nature of your brain. That's when you look at what truly makes sense for your core team—the team that's going to remain after you make the tough decisions associated with your position. You have to decide intellectually what the best decision is for the company. You'll be faced with situations where someone you'll have to let go might be having a baby in four months, and you'll have to not let that emotional decision overrule your intellectual one. If you engage your technical side, you can filter out the noise and decide that when everything is equal between two employees, one is an "A" player and one is a "B" player, and although the "B" player is having a baby, the "B" player has got to go.

It might seem cold, but in this manner, technical and engineering professionals are uniquely suited for leadership positions because of this quality. They're less likely to make those emotional mistakes that lead to bad apples. There is a certain level of necessary detachment that allows you to make the logical decision based on just that: logic. It also makes it easier to own those mistakes.

It did for me.

FULL CIRCLE

I was faced with another hiring situation similar to the one I described earlier—the guy who was shitty to the waitstaff at the restaurant. We relocated a recruit from Seattle who came to us from a competitor. That is to say, he was expensive. He came down for a two-day visit, which put us in a bit of a crunch in terms of making a decision, and we were smack in the middle of our annual financial and head-count planning. As a result, I was pulled away from a lot of the interviews. I didn't get to spend a lot of personal time with him, but in the short time I had, I didn't get that bad gut feeling. The team thought he was a good technical fit, and we ended up hiring him. We relocated him at great expense and paid him a handsome salary.

You can guess what happened next.

He shows up and he's the "me" guy. Everything was about him. My team had two nineteen-inch monitors for each of their computers. He wanted a twenty-seven-inch iMac and a pair of twenty-seven-inch cinema displays. Those displays were approximately $1,800 apiece. Meanwhile, my team's Dell monitors were $300 each.

He stepped in the door feeling entitled because he had come from Amazon, and we had been willing to jump through hoops to get him there. His shit, apparently, did not stink. It took very little time for us to all realize that he had a significant arrogance about him that would never fit in. It took three weeks for me to visit HR and tell them that it wasn't going to work out. They said, "We just spent twenty-five thousand dollars moving this guy here."

I said, "I made the mistake of bringing him here. The bigger mistake is keeping him here."

Can you guess what they said next?

"Can you think of another team where he might fit?" they asked.

Owning my mistake meant accepting the consequences in their entirety. I told them, "No." It had nothing to do with his skills. He hadn't produced a thing at that point. We were still waiting for his monitors from Cupertino. He was still out looking for houses.

Fortunately, he was single and hadn't brought a family with him. Even if he had, he would have had to go. Despite my determination, I still had to go to HR leadership. I met with the same resistance. The next visit was with the CEO. I made my argument that while sending him on his way would be expensive, nothing would be costlier, financially and otherwise, than keeping him here.

The CEO said, "Rob, let him go. It's the right thing to do." He then informed HR that if the employee wanted to move back to Seattle, we'd cover the expense, which of course, was also the right thing to do.

Not surprisingly, the employee took it hard. He went on social media and bad-mouthed us quite a bit, talking about how badly we had treated him. We didn't respond. Frankly, we expected that response. At least, I did. The recruiter came to me with fears that all of his negative posts were going to hurt their recruitment efforts. I assured them that, given time, he would go away. Soon enough, he went back to Seattle, right back to Amazon, and forgot all about us on social media.

It was an expensive mistake, but it was one that was better for everyone. This includes the people who worked for me, all the leaders who served under me, and all those who worked as part of my team. Why? They all saw that, despite the expense, I was willing to own the mistake of bringing him on because I knew his continued presence would have brought down the team.

It's hard to go into those meetings—to have that conversation both with the employee you have to let go and later with your team to own up to your mistake. Not only that, but now you've got to tell your team that a position you sorely need filled is now open again, which means potentially more work for them in the short and maybe even the long term. It also means in order to fill the position, they have to join you in starting the whole process of interviewing and vetting from scratch.

Being a leader shouldn't be easy. I've spoken to so many people who think that once you're a VP or any other higher-level position, life somehow automatically gets easier. While that might be true in a minority of industries, in most cases, nothing could be further from the truth. In actuality, you're now just going to get paid more money to deal with more shit.

Don't let that deter you. Apply your technical brain to owning mistakes, and you'll find that you're making them less often. You'll see how your unique set of skills prepares you to be helpful not only to your team, but to the company as a whole.

In the next chapter, we'll discuss just how important it is to be helpful and the ways in which you can be.

CHAPTER TWO

#BEHELPFUL

It was the first meeting with my newly created social media team and the larger marketing organization within the company. The topic was to determine what campaign we would run for 2009. Of course, the marketing side had all kinds of crazy ideas, all of them thinking each of theirs was genius, all of them doing nothing more than selling our product.

"Why don't we just be helpful?" I asked. "Let's focus all of our content on being helpful to the customers we serve."

Look, I never said my ideas were highly original, but sometimes the simplest ones gain the most traction.

The idea was overrun by the cross talk, twenty-five people in the meeting all shouting over each other. When the meeting eventually ended, the VP of marketing pulled me aside and asked me to expand on the idea of being helpful. I discussed memorable experiences I have had with other companies, and how the ones that I remember were always when someone was doing more than just their job—they were trying to actually help me. He liked the idea and gave me a little budget and a lot of leeway to go run with it.

WHAT DO YOUR CUSTOMERS *REALLY* WANT?

Customers don't want marketing initiatives pushed down their throats. They don't need to hear, over and over again, what you think they want. As such, you must ask them questions to find out what it is they *do* want. If you don't, the chances of your actually selling them anything, let alone the *right* thing, are slim.

"Be helpful" became the mantra of our social media team in conjunction with Rackspace's tagline of Fanatical Support™. We used this refrain to guide the idea that we must think outside the box in order to do the right thing for the customer. This was true even if it wasn't necessarily the right thing for the company or if it in some way broke the rules. It could be the smallest action to the grandest gesture.

In video conferencing with clients, particularly if it was for an issue we needed to fix for them, I made sure to take note of items in the background like books on their shelves and pictures on their desks. If there was a photo of a dog, within a few days of that call they'd receive a bag of dog treats and a note from me.

If a client had an issue on a Saturday night, and we knew the issue meant staying on the phone with us for at least another hour to work through the issue, we'd send a note to a teammate to send pizzas to the customer's location.

People remember the unexpected things you do to help them.

We once had a customer driving from Canada to Austin, Texas, for the South by Southwest (SXSW) festival. We noticed them tweet that their bus had broken down on mile marker forty-seven—or whatever it was—and that they were hungry, thirsty, and waiting for AAA. We convinced a Pizza Hut manager that we were not crazy, and that we did indeed want pizza and sodas delivered to a broken-down RV in the middle of nowhere. The customers were shocked and mentioned us during their talk at the festival.

We were helpful.

People don't forget when you help them. When you go out of your way to be helpful, they will always give you an opportunity to solve their problems, even if you're the problem.

MORE THAN ONE TYPE OF CUSTOMER

As someone from a technical or engineering background, you must remember to be helpful to your internal customers, particularly as you make the move into management. Doing so earns you trust and respect from other teams within the company.

Despite having a large human resources department relative to our number of employees, we struggled to reach our HR representatives for questions. They didn't answer their phones. They (like many of us) were never at their desks. After a number of complaints from my team, I sent an email to the leader of the department detailing our issues. He sent back a scathing response, copying my boss.

My VP always believed in face-to-face meetings, so he brought the three of us together in a room. Once there, I asked the HR leader a simple question: "Who do you work for?"

Immediately he answered that he worked for the CEO. I corrected him.

"You work for me," I told him. "You work for every

employee in this company. You don't work for the CEO. I don't work for the CEO. I work for customers, and I work for our employees."

It was a bold thing to say to him, to be sure. However, not long after that conversation, things improved. In the following months, HR set up kiosks throughout our enormous facility, manned between the hours of 2:00 p.m. and 4:00 p.m. every day. Doing so made an HR representative instantly available to answer any questions the employees might have.

The HR staff was happier because they weren't getting as many complaints. My coworkers and team members were far happier because they didn't have to spend twenty minutes or more to walk over to the HR department in the hopes that someone would be there only to find the offices empty. They knew exactly what time a representative would be at their kiosk, now only fifteen feet away from them.

Being helpful improved the situation on both sides, leaving everyone more satisfied.

GIVE, BUT DON'T EXPECT TO GET

We paid a third-party company for building security. Man the doors, guard the gates—that type of work. One of the company's younger security guards was always so helpful to everyone. He held the doors for staff entering and exiting the building, helped people carry in their packages—always going above and beyond what the company was paying him minimum wage to do.

One day, as he walked to work in the middle of a dense fog, he was hit by a truck. His injuries were severe, and he spent three and a half months in the hospital with no health insurance through his direct employer. He left that hospital without a bill to pay because Rackspace employees contributed so much money to his recovery fund that he never had to pay a penny. His helpfulness, above and beyond what was expected of him, came back to him in a significant way.

As a leader, you have to give without the expectation of getting. It has to be a natural action from you, otherwise it becomes transactional. Be helpful because it is the right thing to do, not because you want something in return.

This is critical when it comes to both former bosses and employees. Why? You never know when either one of them might be a *future* boss.

Throughout my career, I've had to let many people go, largely because of company economics and not poor performance on their part. The same held true for managers.

They were good at their jobs, but the business changed for whatever reasons, and they had to go. Ironically, sometimes a promotion can be the reason. One manager was once given an ultimatum: move to Florida to accept a promotion or part ways with the company. His kids were older, both in high school, and heavily involved in sports. He made the decision to leave the company.

Despite a corporate policy that said we didn't give recommendations for former employees—positive or negative—I immediately helped him look for a new job. He found one without my help. Then, four years later, I recommended him for a role at Rackspace, and we hired him.

Another ex-employee encountered strange circumstances with a job for which he was applying. They required he have a passport for the job, but his was pending. He had been abandoned on the streets of San Antonio at the age of eight, so he didn't have a birth certificate. He didn't know his real last name. A family found him on the streets at the age of twelve—after four years of homelessness—and adopted him.

He feared the interviewers would not believe him regarding his situation, so he asked if I would attend the interview with him to verify that everything was in process. I did it. It was an easy thing to do, and he got the job.

He's now working for the government somewhere, doing things about which he can't tell me.

I know what you're thinking: "Great, Rob. You're a wonderful human being. What does this have to do with preparing me for advancing in my career?"

Being helpful, along with giving without the expectation of getting, are the first steps toward adopting the philosophy of servant leadership.

Don't crawl up the career ladder over the bodies of others. Servant leadership means you recognize and promote the strengths of your employees. You also recognize their weaknesses and address them when you are able. When you do that, your employees push you up the ladder of success.

For example, I had an employee who was a fantastic coder, but he was dyslexic. He could write code with no issues, but he couldn't write legibly or put together a PowerPoint presentation. I needed to ensure that I took him out of any situation where he would be responsible for producing documentation. We worked toward his skillset—the actual coding, the difficult engineering—and got rid of the frivolous tasks that frustrated him, which improved his productivity and interactions with his team. Investing in your employee's strengths is just as meaningful as sending them to conferences or seminars, or paying for tuition, or any of the other things companies routinely do.

gapingvoid
Culture Design Group

@gapingvoid

KNOW WHEN TO BEND THE RULES

A number of years ago, our social media team picked up on the type of tweet you never want to see.

Someone who had applied to the company had been turned down for the job. He posted that he was "just sick of this" and that it was "easier to end it all."

The tweet came in late at night, sometime around 11 p.m. I happened to run the night shift at the time, and I called one of my employees to tell him there was a strong chance we should act on the post. We found his name and then his metadata from the tweet, including his geolocation.

We discovered he was somewhere in northeast Arkansas. By this time, my entire team was up, chatting back and forth via Skype. We found him based on source code he had written and put into a public source code repository using his full name and address. Still, we didn't have his phone number or email address.

We called recruiting in the HR department and got them to pull his file. Not only did we want to use it to obtain his phone number but we wanted to understand our reasons for not selecting him for employment. We found the number for the Department of Public Safety and contacted them, letting them know that we had been made aware of a credible threat of suicide from the individual. They connected us to the local police, who performed a welfare check on him. He was committed for a two-day psychiatric evaluation.

We didn't find that out from the police. Three weeks after the incident, we received a long, heartfelt email from the individual who posted the tweet. He said that he didn't know if he'd have gone through with his ideation that night, but that he had the tools at his disposal, and that thankfully, due to our intervention, he'd never know if he would have done it.

I forwarded the email up to my managers, the CEO, and the chairman of the board. Everybody loved it. We got kudos and high fives on the following Monday when we returned to work.

Then legal heard about it.

The next day I was called into their office and told I was never to do anything like that again—that I put the company at far too much liability. I told them that if I was being told to ignore someone reaching out for help, then fire me now because that was not something I was willing to do. They shot back that if it ever happened again, I *would* be fired.

It did happen again. Twice.

We helped again—and nobody got fired.

HOW DOES THIS APPLY TO GEEKS?

Our social media team always let customers know that if they needed assistance, they could always get ahold of us at help@rackspace.com. As you can see, however, in many situations we've had to think outside the box and take "support" a step further. In the case of the tweeter, we had to use tools that were not provided by our company. We had to do cybersleuthing. We had to do *social forensics* based on the little bit of data we had on the guy, including determining when he'd interviewed and what contact information we'd used to send our "no" response.

If this message had come to the attention of another department without the skillsets that the technical professional (the engineering geek) possesses, I honestly shudder to think about what might have happened to that young man.

It wasn't just about the technical skill, though. If you want to be successful in leadership, you have to understand and accept that most of the rules are written for the least common denominator. They're written for the average team member. Of course, you want your employees to follow the rules ~~99.9 percent~~ most of the time. However, when the time comes for you to make a crucial decision that flies in the face of the rules, particularly when only your unique skillset can solve it, then you must step outside the lines.

I fully recognize that concept feels foreign to your technical brain. We live in a world of absolutes, where numbers don't lie, and breaking rules means programs and applications fail. However, if you are to become a leader who is both successful and fulfilled in your work, you must be prepared for the aberrations and abnormalities that occur with managing and interacting with human beings. People cannot always be effectively led within the structure of the rules.

This is not to say that when you make decisions of this nature that you will always be right.

When I got my offer letter from Rackspace, I replied back to the president of the company—the guy who would be my boss—as well as the chairman of the company. I didn't reply with your standard business email, though; I replied with the ten reasons why they shouldn't hire me.

One of those reasons was that I was going to make mistakes. I wrote that 20 percent of the time, I was going to make the wrong call, although always with the best intentions. What was important, I explained, was that no matter what, I would always learn from that 20 percent. I'd never repeat those mistakes, and I would never fail to admit them to others.

In the next chapter, we'll talk about why it's important to be right 80 percent of the time, but why that 20 percent failure rate is equally crucial to your success as a leader.

—————

CHAPTER THREE

BE RIGHT 80 PERCENT OF THE TIME

When I met Rackspace, I was an independent consultant. I had one kid in college and was making pretty good money at the time. I was working from home, talking to customers from my recliner, and getting paid. My ~~recliner~~ retainer fee kept me comfortable, and I didn't have an excess of customers because frankly, I didn't want a lot of them. I had escaped the corporate world a few years before and I wanted—no, needed—a break, and I wanted more time with my kids.

In this period of comfort, something dawned on me: I was about to have a second kid in college. That nice paycheck suddenly didn't seem so nice. In fact, it was going to be downright insufficient. I needed to make approximately $60,000 more a year, and I needed to ramp up to that quickly. That meant getting my name out more in the San Antonio area so more people knew who I was and would want to work with me.

I called around to about a dozen local tech companies with an offer: if I can get this video tech blogger here to San Antonio to do an interview with your company at no cost to you, will you commit to having a C-level person from your company there for twenty minutes of their time? Not only did they not have to pay to get the blogger there but I also waived my commission to make the arrangements. I ended up with a commitment from seven companies.

Of course, I didn't have the blogger yet.

I followed this guy Robert Scoble, whom I had never met. He was working at Fast Company, where they paid him to interview tech startups. He was heading to Austin for SXSW, an hour and a half away from San Antonio. I called him up and said, "As long as you're in Austin, why don't you come here, and you can meet seven companies in one day?" He wouldn't have to break down his camera gear and move it from company to company. He would be able to see all seven within eight hours.

He said, "No way, South by Southwest is far too busy. Won't happen."

What he didn't know was that a week before, I had discovered that he and his wife would be celebrating their wedding anniversary, and I sent her a $500 gift certificate to a day spa in San Francisco. When he responded "no" via email, I forwarded it to his wife. I said, "It's a shame. I would've really loved to have Robert here."

Thirty minutes later, he called me.

"I guess we're going to San Antonio," he said.

All of a sudden, I've got seven companies, each with three to four people representing them. Public relations teams. CEOs. Marketing. About forty-five people, all told. I was working out of my home and hadn't thought about where we'd actually pull this off. I had no money to spend on a venue because I wasn't charging anyone. I was a Rackspace customer, but I had never spoken with anyone there before. I dialed the 800 number from their website, and they connected me with PR. I told them I needed a room for one day that would hold forty people and had a projector and an internet connection.

Thankfully, they pulled through. Robert, his videographer, Rocky Barbanica, and I showed up to find Rackspace more than ready for our arrival. They had something for everyone—T-shirts, name tags with their company roles, coffee, and Danishes. It was a hell of a lot nicer than I could have made it.

Well, in nine hours, those two guys knocked out all seven videos. At the very end of the day, two men I didn't know came in and watched the last interview. When it was over, they introduced themselves to us. They were the chairman and founder of Rackspace, Graham Weston, and the chief strategy officer, Lew Moorman, who later became the president of Rackspace.

Graham Weston asked us, "What are you guys doing for dinner?"

Robert and Rocky had planned on heading back up to Austin and hadn't booked a hotel locally for that night. One of the companies present for the interviews overheard and put them up for a night in a hotel down on the River Walk. We all met at the hotel bar and had drinks and dinner. Later, Robert and Rocky retired to their room, and I continued to have drinks with the CEO. We talked at length about customer service and taking care of employees. It was a terrific evening.

For the next four months, I had breakfast or lunch once a week with a senior person from Rackspace, either the CEO, president, or some other executive. I'm a little slow on the uptake, so it didn't dawn on me at the time that they were courting me for a full-time position. I met them in March and was hired at the end of June.

In July, Rackspace shared that they had a big announcement, and that they had rented out Austin City Limits, which is a famous music venue. They rented the hall to announce their first-ever acquisitions, two major ones. The chairman of the company asked me if I'd be able to get Robert and Rocky back to film the event. Fast Company saw it as a tech event and sent them out.

Then, in 2008, the tech bubble burst. Fast Company was imploding because the advertising they lived off of dried up overnight. Rocky was laid off. On a whim, I called Lew Moorman, the future president of Rackspace and current chief strategy officer, to see if there was anything we could do. He immediately asked if we could get Scoble as well. He hadn't been laid off, but we were able to get him out of his contract and bring him on as well.

They came in reporting to me, and they began reporting on our outreach to startups, using our resources to tell their stories. The series became so popular that people would turn down a blog post with TechCrunch to land a fifteen-minute video with us. TechCrunch eventually ran our videos.

We did it totally free—not just for our customers, but for

any startups. They could be hosted with any of our competitors. On the website where we posted the videos, I didn't allow marketing to run any advertisements. We spent a good six figures each year on the initiative.

YEAH, BUT SO WHAT?

By now, you're probably thinking about how sore my shoulders must be from patting myself on the back so much. Bear with me. There is a point to all of this.

So many people internally thought the initiative to bring them on to produce these videos was a colossal waste of money and resources. I'd tell them the metrics: the new startup website was getting eighty-five thousand hits a month, which was a significant number at the time. Then they'd counter that it was ineffective because I didn't allow them to run any branding or ads.

They were wrong. Was there marketing? No. Was there Rackspace branding? Absolutely. People knew that we were offering this as a free service to the startup industry. This turned into invitations to mentor at startup incubators like YCombinator and Techstars. We became embedded in the entire startup ecosystem. We created an awareness campaign, and it worked extremely well. We helped little companies that ended up being quite big. We were invited to Washington, D.C., to meet with

President Obama's first ever chief technology officer for the United States.

The point—the "so what"—is this: as an aspiring engineering or technical leader, you have to do something that is likely completely foreign to you. You have to take risks.

Businesses are doing one of three things: dying, doing, or growing. In the tech sector, you can only be doing one of those three things and be seen as successful, and that's growing, particularly if you're in a public company. Public companies in the tech sector are expected to grow more than other nontech companies. For instance, it's not unusual for institutional investors to want to see businesses in the tech sector grow 20 to 25 percent a year, whereas companies in, say, oil or gas are only expected to grow 10 to 15 percent.

In the tech sector, you've always got to be pushing for the next big thing, and the only way you're going to do that is to leapfrog. You have to take jumps of faith in technology. You have to bet on unproven things and invest in unproven technology until it's proven because if you wait too long to do so, then that ship has sailed. You will never be able to catch up with your competitors. They will already be two years ahead of you.

Sometimes the risks will be small. You might be using

JavaScript for your back-end development, but the world seems to be moving over to Node.js. You have to make that consideration before that trend leaves you and your company behind.

Look at data like what the new programmers coming out of college are learning now. What skillset is going to be able to fill your funnel for applicants in the future? You've got to bet that you're going to choose the same things they are so that you have that skilled workforce when you need it.

For the same reason, you need to kill old technology when, quite literally, the people who developed it may now be in leadership roles in your company. They're likely too expensive to be coders anymore. Maybe they've been at the company for fifteen years, and now they're making $185,000 annually. You can replace that person with four coders making $50,000 and using the latest technology.

Additionally, consider that data centers cost tens of millions of dollars to open. Imagine a million-square-foot building filled with tens of thousands of servers—all the power, all the redundancy and cooling. It costs more to cool a data center than to power one, so deciding on where and when you open one is a huge risk. Power is a huge concern for data centers, but I believe they are addressing it well through investing in renewable energy—no matter where the data center is.

The bottom line is that you need to stay on the cutting edge and make the right kinds of gambles. After all, people who are afraid to gamble never win. When was the last time you heard of someone winning the lottery when they didn't buy a ticket? (I include that reference, but to be honest, I never play the lottery.)

Tech companies are infamous for layoffs—often large and often cyclical. Google had a round where they gutted mid-level management. The ones they were getting rid of were those who were complacent. They were happy making their six-figure salary, doing the same thing Monday through Friday. They got their free food in the cafeteria. What they weren't doing was helping Google win. They weren't helping Google grow. Like any other tech company, Google cannot continue to win without growth, and so every few years, they clean house. That was a solid gamble.

Don't get swept out with the rest. Don't be the program manager setting up meetings every day and pulling developers away from their coding just so they can attend them. Be identified as one who is not risk averse. Be the early adopter. Be a little dangerous.

RISK ALIENATION TO MAKE BIG MOVES

Don't fear confrontation.

There will be times when you're going to have to chance alienating your peers, and sometimes even some of your bosses, because you're assigning tasks that are considered risky.

A senior leader came to me and said, "Look, I know you're running social media, but I also know that you can manage developers. I'm going to give you six developers to work in your group. Here is what I want you to work on, but nobody can know about the project."

My team sat in the middle of corporate communications, PR, HR, legal—all of the ancillary groups—yet somehow, I had to keep this all a secret. I went to my boss and asked him to move a particular team away from my group because I needed those specific six chairs. He asked me where I was getting these six people and what they would be working on. I had no choice but to tell him that I couldn't tell him. We had to step on a lot of different teams' toes to get this project done—a project that saved us more than $800,000 a year. We took it out of the hands of people who were playing company politics and losing us money. We rolled out the initiative and essentially said, "Here it is. This is the result of your own inability to get along with each other and work through these problems."

#Saved800K

BIG Moves
WITHOUT RISK
OF ALIENATION
DOESN'T HAPPEN
IN NATURE.

gapingvoid
Culture Design Group

@gapingvoid

Doing so pissed off some of my employees. I had to move them around. They didn't understand why this new team of six was here. They didn't understand why I was spending so much time with them. My boss didn't understand whose budget was being utilized; I had to tell him I didn't know, nor did I care because that wasn't information I was given.

Despite that alienation, taking the chance not only on the initiative but also on alienating the team resulted in massive savings for the company. That just goes to show that although initiatives might feel foreign and go against everything your technical brain thinks, there are always risks worth taking.

It's human nature to be wrong on occasion—in fact, that's inherent to the whole idea of risk. Don't be wrong 20 percent of the time about the things that matter, however.

This concept might seem quite obvious, but common sense isn't always so common, especially in business and particularly in leadership. I once bet wrongly on a service platform that cost us more time than actual money. But since money was time, it was costly.

You must do your due diligence in assessing a risky move. Having said that, at some point you have to say it's done. If you spend another week to make the decision, that week could result in a lost opportunity. That's where experience comes in. You have to trust yours. If you've done the right amount of diligence and the risk level is within your pain threshold—whether it's financial or whatever the case may be—you've got to pull the trigger. You can't take every decision up to the C-suite guys. If you ascend to the position of director or VP, you are being paid to make decisions. Make them.

HOW DO YOU CONVINCE THEM YOU'RE RIGHT?

Bringing on the guys from Fast Company was a million-dollar bet, as that's what the annual cost of the project was. The foundation for that gamble had been laid in the way that I interacted with the senior leaders when they were first taking me to lunch, wooing me to come work for them. I didn't treat them like bosses. They were just other tech guys from San Antonio. I wasn't looking to work for them and never thought I would, so I could be really blunt in our interactions. As a customer, I could tell from my own experience what I thought they sucked at, what they were really good at, and where they were just missing the boat. I felt comfortable telling them the blunt truth without the fear of whether or not they were going to like it.

Trust, a solid track record, integrity, and honesty are the things you need your senior leaders to see in you in order to take advantage of the risky opportunities that present themselves. Doing so allows you to deliver that essential, brutal honesty that allows you to get shit done.

In the next chapter, we'll talk about the best ways to talk to your senior leadership so that you can do just that.

CHAPTER FOUR

HOW TO TALK TO SENIOR LEADERS

@gapingvoid

Have you ever heard of a bus duct? No? I didn't think so.

Like so many things we've never heard of, though, bus ducts serve an extremely important purpose. They are essentially giant fuses, approximately three-feet-long, solid-copper elements weighing hundreds of pounds. They conduct the massive amounts of power going through a data center.

"That's great, Rob. Nobody cares."

Under any other circumstance, you'd be right. As long as you can access your Amazon account or log in to your work intranet while you're pretending to work from home, nobody gives a rat's ass about bus ducts because they never fail. They never blow.

Except one did—in Rackspace's largest data center in Dallas-Fort Worth. That particular data center hosted hundreds of thousands of websites—many of your favorites, your most used and visited.

We were down for almost twelve hours. And no, they don't sell bus ducts at your local Radio Shack (RIP Radio Shack).

As you can imagine, we had some unhappy customers. Our incoming customer service calls ramped up exponentially. Our social media hits went from seven thousand a week to over two hundred thousand in a matter of hours.

Worse yet, I got word that TechCrunch was preparing to post a blog entitled "The Dead Zone Data Center." I had a good relationship with the founder, Mike Arrington, who gave me a heads-up they were going to run the article. While I couldn't talk him out of posting it, I convinced them to go with a less ominous title, going with the more flippant "Who Tripped over the Power Cord?" They weren't going to pull the article because they utilized a project management software internally called Basecamp. Want to take a guess where Basecamp hosted their data?

Our initial release was along the lines of what you'd expect. We said, "We're aware of outages related to our Fort Worth data center. More details to come." Just the right amount of sparse information and cold delivery to infuriate any consumer. Anyone who's had their residential internet go down for a significant length of time without some type of explanation immediately looks to the competitor to change their service. Our customers, particularly without the storage space to move them to one of our other data centers, would look to do the same if we didn't do things differently.

Every time there was an incident, minor or major, we had an escalating incident management call. The number of people on the call depended on the severity of the occurrence. In this case, we had forty individuals: the CEO, the head of operations, the heads of the data center, public relations, and sales, as there was no doubt this incident could affect our sales moving forward.

I wanted us to get out in front of the news. Write a blog post, go public on social media, explain to our customers and the general public exactly what was happening, what a bus duct was, why we didn't have a spare, all of it. Complete transparency.

As you might expect, there was pushback, particularly from the finance and legal departments. Just how much liability you admit to depends on how much financial liability you've got, and they didn't feel we had enough information to say anything publicly without putting ourselves at significant risk. Their objections did not fall on deaf ears, particularly those of the CEO.

We were being lambasted on our social media accounts. Our followers crushed us for being silent almost as much as they did for the servers being down. Based on the number of customers who threatened to leave our service based on our lack of response, we stood to lose, easily, millions of dollars.

I had to make a choice. Instead of continuing to talk to our CEO via conference call, I walked into his office, muted my line, and asked him to do the same. When he did so, I asked him: "How do you want the Band-Aid pulled off? Slow or quick? I want it pulled off fast. Let's get the hurt over with."

I asked him what it could hurt to release an explanatory

video. The first law of medicine is "Do no harm," and the same thing is true in crisis management. We were going to explain to our customers what happened—we would have to do that anyway—but if we did it in the traditional way, it would take three months after tons of meetings resulting in fifty pages of justifications and confusing diagrams. We needed to just get the explanation out there.

Our CEO unmuted his line. He said, "I think we need to get in front of this. Rob's already worked it out."

In HR, we had our own internal videography group who filmed things for internal use—work anniversaries, birthdays, and the like. My team and I grabbed them and took them to a meeting room where there was a whiteboard. We walked through the setup with the CEO a few times— what he should draw, what he should say, and how he should explain it. We managed to get it all in a couple of cuts. Within an hour, we uploaded it to YouTube and shared the link on our social media accounts.

The uproar drastically dropped. People understood what we were doing. They saw that we weren't running around like chickens with our heads cut off, and that there was an actual cause. We knew how to solve it, and we were working on the remedy. It didn't mean they were happy with us. We still lost a number of customers over the incident, but we gained most of them back over the course of the year. Offering that transparency renewed some of their initial confidence in us. One of our East Coast competitors posted a blog commending our openness in the face of adversity. We would not have been able to provide that clarity, however, if I didn't know how to talk to leadership.

YOU CAN'T BE A GREAT LEADER AND A WALLFLOWER

gapingvoid
Culture Design Group

@gapingvoid

LEADERS WANT YOUR OPINION

In talking to senior leaders, you must get them focused. More often than not, you're going to have multiple people in a room, all with their own opinions, most of them wrong. Many will err on the side of:

"Do nothing."

"Everything has to go through legal for approval."

"Stop responding on social media."

There will be times when it takes going to the opposite end of the spectrum to find the right solution. Instead of hiding behind standard operating procedures, in this case we needed to open the kimono as quickly as possible.

Getting the CEO to focus on a singular quiet, calm, and rational conversation instead of people quite literally screaming into the phone is the most effective way to communicate with leadership during a crisis.

Senior leadership will move or has moved you into a management role because you're smart. Whether they admit it or not, they've done this because you just might be smarter than they are, at least when it comes to certain topics. You are the subject-matter expert about something you understand better than your leadership does. They want you to talk to them about the things about which you're the most knowledgeable and passionate. They want your opinion. Leaders want someone that they're comfortable with waking them up in the middle of the night with a crisis call because they know they wouldn't if it wasn't absolutely necessary.

You have to return that trust in them by believing in them enough to disagree with them, even vehemently at times. Now, common sense has to come into play here. You don't want to come in guns blazing with, "I'm right and you're wrong." That's essentially telling them, "I'm smart and you're stupid." That is not a recommended tactic, and I'll deny it if you blame me.

That said, there were times when I completely disagreed with my leadership, and I let them know. It isn't enough to just tell them, though; you have to tell them *why*. Make your arguments using that subject-matter expertise you possess. If they come back and tell you, "Sorry, but this is the way it's going to be," then there are times when you have to accept it and move on. Never let that be a reason not to voice your objections.

We called ourselves "Rackers" at Rackspace. I don't know who coined it, but it was just an employee thing. Sometime after the company went public, we copyrighted the term.

Then the legal department began cracking down on any employee that used "Racker" in their Twitter handles or in their blog posts. They told them they had to use the trademark symbol next to the term if they wanted to use it.

I was pissed. Rackers was how we self-identified. In my opinion, it wasn't owned by the company but by the employees. I understood trademarking it for protection, but legal was using it to corral the actions of what employees were saying on their personal blogs, websites, and social media accounts, and I felt that was flat-out wrong.

I sent an email to the CEO, the heads of legal and HR, and my direct supervisors. It said that the requirement was ridiculous, and we wouldn't stand for it. *We were Rackers.* Did they want to destroy the moral fiber and culture that helped build this company? Did they want to turn this into an IBM? There's a reason you don't hear people walking around saying they're an "IBM-er" or a "Dell-er." They don't have that same pride, that same affinity for their company that Rackers do. Rackers feel as though they built the company together. Don't take that feeling away.

In the end, the Rackers prevailed. We were able to use the term without that ridiculous trademark symbol unless, of course, we were posting on the official Rackspace blog. The second head of legal even sent me an email telling me how much he agreed with me. He told me to stay on his boss's ass about it. We actually got the internal policy changed before it became a huge uproar in the company—which it would have been—all from trusting leadership to hear and value my opinion.

DON'T BE A YES-PERSON

Confidence is key, but so is respect.

Being a yes-person will only get you somewhere in one situation: if you work for a boss who is *also* a yes-person. Yes-people generally aren't hiring people smarter than them. They're hiring people who they feel won't present a threat to them—to their position, to their budget responsibilities, or to their fiefdom. Yes-people tend to hire yes-people.

Real technology leaders despise yes-people because we are in a thinking industry. We pay people to be creative. It does no one any good if all of your creative thoughts stay swirling around in your head. If you're the wallflower sitting in a meeting with a brilliant idea that would save the company money and time compared to the plan of action they want to implement, then you're doing *everyone* a disservice, including yourself.

It is for this reason that being an approachable leader is also important. Not only do you not want to be a yes-person as you move into leadership, but you don't want to foster an environment where your employees feel they have to be yes-men and yes-women in order to survive. They need to feel comfortable disagreeing with the boss even in mixed company. It is always easier to disagree with a boss one-on-one. It is much more challenging to do so if he's in a meeting with his peers.

When critical situations present themselves, as a manager

you have to have or find the cojones to say, "Wait. Stop. You're being stupid right now," without of course *actually* telling them they're being stupid. Some key phrases to use are:

"Hear me out for a second."

"I might suggest an alternative solution."

"Have we considered this?"

As a manager, I've lost count of the number of times I've been in meetings with staff and had someone pull me aside after the meeting with what was a terrific idea when all the right people were no longer in the room to make the decision. Then it becomes necessary to reconvene the meeting or discuss it via email, which leads to wasted time and more complicated communication.

Don't be that person. Good leaders understand that their employees have more to teach them than they've got to teach their employees. Trust that your superiors know that, and make sure that those who work for you know that as well.

YOU DON'T DO THIS ALONE

As a tech geek, you're used to solitude. You're far more

comfortable keeping your head down, getting lost in code, and getting your job done. As we've already mentioned, if you're exceptionally good at what you do, you're going to move up the chain. If you're reading this book, there's a good chance you actually want that to happen, but you realize that doing this requires pushing out of your comfort zone.

The good news is that if vertical movement in your career is something you truly want, you don't have to maintain your solitary nature to do it. In fact, you have to shed that way of thinking if you want to advance. Not only do you need to learn how to talk to leadership above you, but you've got to know how to get both your peers and your eventual leaders to help you along the way.

In the next chapter, we'll talk about how you do that.

CHAPTER FIVE

GET PUSHED UP THE LADDER, BUT DON'T FORGET TO PULL

gapingvoid®
Culture Design Group

@gapingvoid

One of our CEOs decided to leave the company after a fifteen-year tenure. As a publicly traded company, we had to do our due diligence to find a replacement. It made sense to perform a public search.

However, the search went long. Too long. Of course, the longer it takes, the more expensive it gets. A number of people came to me asking why we weren't hiring Taylor. They all thought he was the natural fit as the next CEO. He was a longtime employee, had grown through the ranks, and brought experience as a Marine officer.

I took all of that feedback and visited the chairman of the board at Rackspace. He was acting as the CEO at the time, a position he did not want to occupy permanently. He knew it and so did I. He had been the CEO prior to becoming chairman, and he had served in the role on an interim basis once before.

"People want a Racker in this position," I told him. They didn't want someone from the outside, particularly because we had been looking at candidates from industries that, frankly, we didn't respect such as CenturyLink and Time Warner Cable. These were internet companies that didn't operate in the way we did internet. We weren't a service provider—we were a hosting company. There is a big difference between providing the pipes and building and running the data centers.

I told the chairman that Taylor was the right candidate, and that the majority of my team agreed. Not only that, but people outside of my team were coming to me and saying the same. He thanked me for my opinion and told me he agreed. I wasn't content with that.

"How can I help you make this happen?" I asked him.

He advised me to email the board because the decision would ultimately come from them. The issue there was that the board was nonemployees. They're people who work for Bing & Company or Yahoo!. I got the list of their names and email addresses and sent them personalized messages telling them why we felt Taylor was the right Racker for the job. I made sure to use that term often because it was important to us that they knew he was one of us.

While I have no idea just how much influence those emails had, Taylor was announced as our CEO three weeks later.

In my mind, there was nothing out of the ordinary with my going to the board of directors. They exist to make decisions in the best interest of the company and its shareholders, which includes the employees. I thought what I was doing was giving them better information to make a more informed decision.

Taylor had been CEO for about six weeks when it came up in conversation that I had emailed the board recommending him for the position. He was shocked. He thought it was crazy. I thought it was my responsibility.

Sometime later, Taylor promoted me to vice president. He made it crystal clear to me that it was not an "exchange" for my campaign for him. He based it on the work I had done leading what he called our "Special Forces"—the social media team that had built out a new way of listening to and engaging our customers. He felt I deserved the title.

A believer in asking for what you want, I also asked for the promotion. Again, doing so was not an "I scratched your back, you scratch mine" situation. I had been at the company for seven years as a director and was still in that position. My pay had increased as well as my responsibilities, but truthfully, it was on my bucket list to be a VP at a publicly traded company.

Taylor agreed that I met all of the qualifications, and in the same way I had helped push him up the ladder, he did the same for me.

BUSINESS IS THE ART OF GETTING SOMEONE WHERE THEY NEED TO BE, FASTER THAN THEY WOULD GET THERE WITHOUT YOU.

Culture Design Group

@gapingvoid

Everyone likes to see family members do well. If your brother gets a promotion, you're happy for him. It's the same way at a company—at least it is if it has the same culture as the one that exists at Rackspace. You want to see your own do well. We didn't want to see someone come in from outside the company. Everyone wanted to see a Racker in that role.

For morale reasons, it is critically important for the culture of a corporation to see people from within the company moving up into senior roles. There was a time when Rackspace made a huge mistake during a growth spurt in 2006. They couldn't internally raise mid-level managers fast enough, so they started hiring them from the banking industry. Next thing we know, we had this layer of managers who were competent, but they weren't part of the family.

They were seen only as "the boss," and that's exactly what they were, through no fault of their own. They came from industries completely different from ours, and they didn't know how to manage people within our culture. They had no clue what servant leadership was; if you used that phrase, you'd see their eyes travel to the back of their head.

Their biggest problem was that they weren't leaders, and they certainly weren't servant leaders. It's rare when you can bring leaders in from the outside that can be truly impactful. It's not enough for them to know and learn the financials of the company; they need to know the folklore. Stories like the married couple who were caught in the executive conference room in a compromising position by security one night. The stories that make a Racker a Racker or a Zappos employee a Zappotonian. That is how you keep a company culture together instead of turning it into a factory.

Technology changes so quickly that employees have to learn a new skillset every year just to keep up. Invest in their learning. Give them the time to do it. Understand that there are times when you might need to grant an employee a third of the time in their week for learning new skills instead of building the current program because it will keep them moving forward in the long term. It will also keep them interested and engaged because technical people never stop learning. Give people purpose and autonomy, and they will succeed.

BE CHARLIE

There is a saying that our chairman/CEO came up with. It was written all over our offices. I've found this quote incredibly motivating as a leader, and I hope you will as well as you ascend into a similar role.

> "What people want is to be a valued member of a winning team on an inspiring mission."

You want your employees to know that as important as they are to the company, they're also important to you personally. When I joined Rackspace, I did it with the intention of somehow contributing to changing the world. I had done that once in my involvement with the creation of Wi-Fi, and I wanted to do it again. I used that mission to inspire my team to want to do the same.

When your team feels that kind of energy exuding from you, they suck it right up. They feed off your energy. Nobody wants to work for the pointy-haired boss in Dilbert. He's what I call an asshat. No energy.

Be Charlie, my old boss from Radio Shack.

The man stood all of about four feet, and he had a fake front tooth. Once, we were attending a team meeting with all of the Radio Shack managers in the district. Every time Charlie got excited about something, he would accidentally spit that tooth across the room. Now, I know that sounds gross and over the top, but it illustrates a point.

Charlie was alive. He was passionate about what he did.

Those are the kind of people you want both above and below you. If you're the man in the middle, you need to both push and pull others up along the way. Helping employees win makes them want you to win, and this will naturally push you up the ladder.

REPLACE YOURSELF

This is especially important in a fast-growing company. We're not talking about an upholstery firm where the jobs don't change very often and where the bosses are there for thirty years or more. We are talking about the tech industry, where there is always room for upward mobility for a person with the right attitude, the right intelligence, and the right drive. No leader in the tech world should fear training an employee so well that they replace them and cause them to lose their job.

That's how it works.

If you are smart enough to train someone to do your job that means you are smart enough to go do someone else's job. Speaking generally, that move isn't a lateral shift; it's an upward one. You might stay a director, but now you're a director of a team that's much larger, with a great deal more budget authority. Along with that increased responsibility comes an increased salary. Not all directors are paid the same.

As a manager, I was always looking for my replacement. I once hired someone to run the social media team for me, the only team I actually had at the time. Like our CEO, he was already a Racker, but I brought him in from another team. I knew right away that he would take my place in running the daily operations of the social media team. This meant, however, that I didn't know what I was going to do for my next step.

I began to look at social marketing and began working with their team, which did not report to mine. They reported to the marketing department. As I worked more and more with them, the company, and the marketing team, I saw that it was a better fit for me to work with them. So they moved the entire team to work under me, giving me a manager of social media and a manager of social marketing. I replaced myself, and I added additional responsibility.

I grew.

Even though hiring and training those employees didn't push me up to the next level, it drastically expanded my role and my influence throughout the company because along with any marketing team comes money—a lot of it. Companies spend crazy amounts of cash on marketing, more than I could believe was possible until I started getting a cut of it.

It was around this time that I was also able to acquire the team of developers for the "black project" that I was tasked with earlier in the book, gained more trust, and was given more responsibility. I was promoted to VP and took over an office in San Francisco, where I led a mix of creatives and marketers.

There, I continued to train up my employees to assume more and more of the responsibilities of my job so that I had more time to invest in and investigate things to help advance our teams as well as the company. To do so, I had to pick someone in the San Francisco office and say, "I'm the boss of the office, but you manage the office. Everyday decisions are yours."

If the soda machine was empty, I didn't get a call. If the rent on the building wasn't paid, I didn't get a call. She got the bump to managing the office, which put her on a path of continual upward growth. As I pulled her up the ladder, so too would she push me up that same path when the time came for her to replace me.

Do not fear replacing yourself. If you're the best developer on your team, coach up those around you so that when the time comes for opportunities to move forward, they champion you for the position the way we did for our CEO. Doing so also alleviates you of the guilt of leaving your team without your programming and development skillsets because you will have trained someone effectively enough to take your place. Your team will be stronger for it.

BE FRIENDS WITH YOUR EMPLOYEES

I've never been one to shy away from a little bit of controversy. I'm not going to start doing that here.

I've always gotten a good deal of pushback, especially in the tech sector, about championing the notion that not only *can* you be friends with your employees, but you *should*.

Many people see this idea as binary. Zero or one. It's on or it's off. The problem with that is people aren't binary. They aren't exclusively one thing or the other. People have bad days, whether they are employees or leaders. They've got kids, and soccer practices, and strep throat, and holiday concerts, or they realized that morning that their driver's license expired.

As a leader, get to know your employees. To be fair, some employees may not want that. Some people hold true to a separation of work and personal life and therefore won't share. I'm not advocating that you sneak down to HR and snoop around in their files. At the same time, don't hesitate if an employee invites you over for dinner, a pool party, or to watch the football game on Sunday. Take that as an opportunity to find out who they are outside of their work persona.

I've worked with a number of leaders who believe mixing work and pleasure is wrong. I wholeheartedly agree that any kind of romantic relationship with anybody in your food chain is absolutely wrong. I'm not disputing that. Fostering a friendly relationship with your employees, however, allows you to learn what's really important to them and, as such, what motivates them.

Be it their hobbies, travel, or their love of the arts, you will find something out about what drives them that you won't find out on an annual review form. If all you know about your employees is where they see themselves in two years, then all you *really* know about them is what they think you want to hear as the answer to that question. It will be something work related and likely false. You won't learn that, in truth, they'd like to be independently wealthy, travel the world, and collect Mayan pottery.

Make them comfortable enough with you that on that annual review they can tell you that they don't want to be working there in two years. That's equally useful information for you. While it shouldn't be motivation for you to care any less about their development, it also allows you to dedicate your resources to grooming someone who *does* have an interest in being with the company in the next two years and beyond. You'll still be sure that person gets their deserved pay raises and the like, but now you know their ambitions, which is a crucial piece of information for you and your team.

CRACK THE SHELL

As before, I understand how difficult and intimidating the idea of this kind of relationship building can be. You prefer the comfort of your cubicle cave, plugged into your music, coding to your geeky heart's content, happy to be left alone. If you are going to ascend, take on more responsibility, and make more money, you are going to have to come out of your shell and help others do the same.

One of the guys on my team was an avid gamer. The only time he came out of his shell was when he was playing video games. We had PlayStations, Xboxes, and old-style stand-up pinball games and arcade cabinets all over the office. We'd have tournaments and prizes for the winners.

We also had a culture of giving back to the community. Every employee got three days a year to go and volunteer for whatever they wanted to do—any nonprofit they wanted. They weren't required to get a piece of paper signed saying they were there for eight hours. If they wanted to do it, they were paid to do so on top of their allotted vacation days.

I knew this guy had amazing potential if I could just get him out of his cave, so I encouraged him to find a way to utilize his passion for video games. He ended up organizing what has now become a national event at Rackspace. In fact, it's been so popular that they've had up to five hundred people participate. They build giant temporary networks that allow them to bring their consoles in for plug-in-and-play marathon sessions. Similar to the fundraisers where someone pledges a certain amount of money per mile, they get donors to give for every hour of gameplay. They raised close to $100,000 for their charity of choice.

Organizing the charity game-a-thon forced him to break out. He had to promote it for the event to be a success, and promote it he did. It's a nationwide league. They have an annual conference where he has to speak. He still has the tendency to go back to his desk and put the white earbuds in, but the truth is the experience has made him a better employee in almost every way imaginable.

More people know who he is. Now, they know more about his skillsets beyond gaming—his internal skillset. He's more approachable. He's more likely to see someone walk by and pull an earbud out to talk to them instead of keeping his head down. He's more confident and comfortable when speaking in front of other people. In fact, I could rely on him to speak up in a meeting when his input was needed.

Think about this: if you have ten employees and manage that kind of result with all ten of them, you suddenly have an incredible team on your hands. When people see that incredible team, they look at their leader and say, "That must be an awesome leader."

Pull people up as you climb, and you'll find the ones you're pulling will give you that push.

THEY'LL THANK YOU FOR IT

After Taylor was named CEO, many people thanked me privately for approaching the board with our collective desire to see him in the role. Of course, some were appreciative for different reasons. The CFO didn't want to do another earnings call without a CEO with him. The interim CEO didn't want to be CEO. Everyone had a different motivation.

The biggest reason? Taylor ended up being a great CEO. When Rackspace was about to be acquired by a large telecommunications company, he looked at the deal and saw the number of employees they told him would have to be cut. He went into a room full of investment bankers, the chairman of the board, and the board of directors and said, "I can't sign this because it's just not the right thing for us to do."

The chairman pulled him out of the meeting, and they talked. When they went back in, together they told the rest that there was no way to move forward with the deal.

Less than three months later, Taylor held an open-house meeting for directors and above. Normally for these events he's onstage wearing a wireless mic, and everyone is sitting in neat little rows. This time we walked in the room, and all the chairs were in a circle around a single chair in the center of the room. Taylor came in and sat in that chair. He told the story of that meeting where they refused to sell the company. He cried as he spoke. It was so emotional for him. Just as we had stood up and said, "He's our guy," he had turned around and done the same for us.

Roughly eighteen months later, Rackspace did sell to a private equity firm, but for a much different kind of deal. Equity firms don't bring redundant positions with them, so the employee losses were minimal. It also immediately vested the stock options for all the employees, which was great financially for almost everyone. Someone could have been at Rackspace for a month on a four-year vesting schedule, and now they're 100 percent vested and could sell their stock tomorrow. Truth be told, a lot of millionaires were made that day. Those millionaires are still in San Antonio, reinvesting in new startups and doing incredible things for our city.

As a company we pushed for one of our own, and he lifted us all with his rising tide.

THE RIGHT PEOPLE, THE RIGHT TOOLS

It was clear to us that Taylor was the right fit for the job, and it is terrific when things work out in that manner. Trying to find the right people for the right job can be unpredictable and challenging because people themselves are unpredictable and challenging. As important as it is to find the right people to replace you, it's also important that when faced with certain challenges, you also have the right tools for the job, whatever those tools might be.

In the next chapter, we will look at what that means, particularly through the lens of the tech-geek brain.

CHAPTER SIX

DO YOU WANT A DRILL OR A HOLE?

From 1985 to 1988, I managed a Radio Shack in Marin County, California. It was wine country, a gorgeous place. We had the most interesting customers. Industrial Light & Magic was just down the road from us. Robin Williams came in to buy gag gifts for his mother, who had a home nearby in Santa Rosa. Francis Ford Coppola's winery and estate were only a few miles away, and he would stop in from time to time as well.

Name-droppy enough for you?

This is all to say that with that level of clientele, even though it was a Radio Shack, we had to run a tight ship. We did. At twenty-four years old, I had doubled the profits of the store in a year as compared to the results of the previous manager. In fact, I almost never saw my district manager. He was responsible for almost eighty stores in the Bay Area and spent the majority of his time dealing with his "problem children."

Of course, then, the one day he visited my store, I screwed up.

He had come in to look at my merchandising and check inventory levels—typical district manager responsibilities. While he was up front inspecting a display, a customer came in and asked me if we sold drills. My immediate response was, "No, I'm sorry, but there is an Ace Hardware a couple of miles up the road." He thanked me and headed for the door, passing my district manager, who had heard the conversation. He followed the customer outside.

The next thing I knew, they walked back in together. My manager took him over to a display on the wall where we had an assortment of tools. One of them was an awl, essentially a metal rod to be used with a hammer (or a fist) to punch a hole in a wall, for the low, low price of $1.79. My district manager handed it to the customer and then pointed to me.

"He'll ring you up," he said. When the man left, my manager pulled me aside.

"You know what you did wrong there? You asked him what he wanted, but you didn't ask him what he needed. What he needed was a hole. We sell things that make holes. We sold him the awl. We just made ninety-five cents on that sale. Don't always trust what a customer asks for because sometimes even they don't know what they truly need. That guy thought the only way he could make the hole he needed was with a drill. Sure, a drill will make that hole, but so will something a whole lot cheaper."

I'll admit, I was somewhat stunned. It's because of that that I recall the lesson so vividly. I was thinking, but I wasn't thinking—or listening—all the way.

I made an assumption that the customer knew what he wanted. He asked for a drill, so it must have been what he needed. My district manager took the time, which was really no time at all, to dig just a little bit deeper, to understand his actual need, and the customer walked away with something that fulfilled his need and saved him money.

THE JOB OF THE LEADER
IS TO DISCOVER WHAT'S
ALREADY THERE

RIGHT TOOL, RIGHT JOB, RIGHT TIME

This lesson applies to you, the tech geek moving toward management, in a number of ways.

One of the things I hear that I don't like at all, often in the technology space, is that if your only tool is a hammer, everything you see is a nail. The reason I don't like it is because it's true. It points to a pervasive short-sightedness. For example, for someone who works in marketing, the hammer they use is the money in their budget. The way they improve product visibility is to spend more money. That's the tool they know how to use.

As a result, instead of focusing on how to make better use of their hammer by using it in different ways, the marketing team focuses on getting more (and bigger) hammers because that's how they know how to operate.

Still, every year, it's not uncommon to see the marketing budget grow almost as fast as the company does. If the company is growing 20 percent a year, the marketing budget typically grows at the same rate. I am guilty of this as well—I'll spend the budget I am given.

Another phrase I can't stand is that the customer is always right. I wholeheartedly disagree. I believe customers can and should be fired for a variety of reasons.

Abuse my staff? You're fired. We can't make money off of you because you're too needy? You're fired. You're too indecisive, so we can't satisfy you because you keep changing your mind? Guess what? You're fired. I always loved handing those types of customers over to my competitors. Let them deal with that problem. Like really—hand that problem off.

It's the same reason I have no qualms firing problem employees, and you shouldn't either. Let one of your competitors hire them. Let them waste production cycles and dollars trying to manage that. Don't let that be your problem.

So often, customers call because they have an idea for a website. They're sure it's going to be huge, the "next big thing." They wanted to come in and get eight servers with load balancers. They wanted to overbuild the hell out of their system based on growth they were sure was coming, which is an absolutely foolhardy way to spend your investor dollars.

Would it have been a short-term win for our company financially? Sure. For three months, we could have taken a lot of money from those people. In three months, however, they would run out of that money, blame us for overselling them, and move on to a competitor on one server—something we probably told them to do in the first place.

Sometimes you have to educate the customers that they don't need to go out and buy the $79 Black and Decker drill. Let's start with an awl and make a hole. You can always upgrade to the drill later. Starting with the awl only requires an investment of a dollar and some change, so you're not going to lose much by upgrading to a drill. In the same sense, it's easier to upsize things in infrastructure like servers and load balancers. It's always easier to upsize than downsize. The same holds true with staffing.

Downsizing is always painful and expensive, whether with physical infrastructure or employees.

WHAT IS THE REAL PROBLEM YOU WANT TO SOLVE?

We recently drove to Florida for my daughter's wedding,

and instead of using the GPS that came standard with my Audi, I used Waze, an amazing GPS application. Why? It's better. The problem Waze was initially trying to solve was getting real-time traffic flow information into the hands of the general consumer—that is, information about road construction, unexpected closures, stoplights out, and so forth.

What's incredible is that it's become so much more than that now. On our drive, we'd get a notification that a truck was broken down on the side of the road more than half a mile ahead, allowing us to adjust our route or lane if necessary. Plus, every time it told us a police officer was on our route, it was almost never wrong because the app used crowd-sourced information to provide the real-time updates.

The founders of Waze likely never imagined that it would compete against companies like Magellan and TomTom, which once owned the GPS market, but it does. Waze is often more specific and accurate than the applications built into some luxury cars. Waze is certainly better than what Audi delivers to me.

Instead of sticking to their original design of updating traffic flow information—which was useful but not the real problem for consumers—they solved a problem that many drivers had, which was having an updated navigation system that gave them information as it happened. In doing so, they became a major player in the GPS market, with their technology eventually being bought by Google to add to its Maps functionality in 2013.*

SOLVE–DON'T CREATE

In solving for *real* problems, be sure that you don't create problems via micromanagement.

We established earlier that rules were made for the least common denominator: people who aren't able to think for themselves, so they need written guidelines like washing your hands when you return from the restroom if you work in food service. We'd like to think that everyone knows that as a matter of common sense, and yet there that sign is, required by law, in just about every bathroom in the United States.

Rules are made at any company for a variety of reasons. Some of them are for legal reasons, such as rules that prohibit firearms in the building, to protect both the company and the employees. That's a valid rule. Other rules are made to protect territory, turf, and budgets. They're to protect from encroachment by the enemy, like the beach-

---

* https://techcrunch.com/2013/06/11/its-official-google-buys-waze-giving-a-social-data-boost-to-its-location-and-mapping-business/

heads at Normandy with the big concrete tank busters and the spools of wire.

The problem with surrounding yourself with these defensive measures is that in doing so, you're now closing yourself off from the rest of the corporation in a way. You're preventing access to people, knowledge, and potential partnerships that could be valuable to you and could do more to protect your "turf" than some silly rules can—rules that are absolutely nonsensical when you look at them.

I had a boss whose rule was that everyone had to be in the office at 9:00 a.m. every morning, no matter what. Once, while he was on vacation, we had a sleet storm in San Antonio. We don't get ice in San Antonio very often. We don't get sleet unless shit gets weird. Hence, we don't know how to drive on it. It literally snows here every quarter century. When it does, the mayor gets on television and says that anyone caught on the highway will be arrested.

I called every department head and told them to inform their staff that if it's not safe for them to get to work, they stay home and work from there. It's the internet age, and we're talking programmers and marketers. Almost every one of us would have been able to work from home for a day.

Around 2:00 p.m., I get a call from my boss who got wind, even while on vacation, that I shut the office down. He was upset that the main office in Florida would come down on him for the office being closed on account of a little bit of ice. Floridians don't drive in the ice either. The opposite happened: not only were they not upset but they commended the move. Still, my boss was insistent that it was the wrong move. In the office every day by 9:00 a.m. That was the rule.

That rule didn't mean anything. It didn't improve productivity. It didn't improve morale. It didn't improve safety, and it certainly didn't improve production, particularly for the programmers. Coders and engineers get on rolls where they're working and when they next look up, it's four thirty in the morning. They've been there all night working nonstop. They might go home and crash or they might just sleep on the floor in their office. Do you actually expect them to be awake, alert, and ready to go again at 9:00 a.m.? Or do you let them sleep until noon, wake up refreshed, and give you another fourteen hours' worth of work on *their* schedule, the way *their* brain works?

I prefer to follow how their brains work and not mine. I trust them.

Publishing on the corporate blog was also surrounded by nonsensical rules. There were so many layers of approval that by the time an article was given a green light, the content was stale and no longer mattered, whereas it would have been meaningful had we been able to post it that day or the one following. Instead, we wasted time and money to go through hoops to get everyone from sales, to marketing, to legal, to branding, to God Almighty to look at some story about employees getting together to paint a local junior high school during the summer.

As a tech geek, you are likely one of the most detail-oriented people you know. Engineers are precise human beings. While attention to detail is always a good thing, it can lead to the slippery slope of micromanagement if you're not careful. It's hard to give up that precision, that need to have your hand in everything because you know, *just know*, that without your oversight, someone is going to screw something up.

If you are going to move into a leadership position, you have to let that go. Hire grown-ups, people you can tell what you expect from them in their position and then leave them the hell alone. Don't bring someone onto your team to do their job and pay them for it. Hire them to do the job you need them to do—the job you are expected to do. Hire help.

Micromanagement isn't just a problem for you; it can also be a problem for your employees, particularly those who don't need it. If they need it, then micromanage their ass out the door. If they don't, however, then your constant need to look over their shoulder, double-checking their work, sends them a negative message. It tells them that you don't trust them. It forces them to ask themselves what value they're adding if you always have to review their work. They will question why they are even on the team. That feeling does not lead to a productive, happy employee—one who you can develop or that will push you up the ladder.

The right solution—the right person that owns the right tool for the right job—prevents the need for micromanagement.

We had quarterly engagement surveys in which employees would rate their direct managers and their senior leadership all the way up to the CEO. They measured how engaged employees were with their leaders and how well they thought leadership as a whole was performing.

As a survey given to about six thousand employees, there was a significant expense to collating that data and interpreting it. As you can imagine, the results were taken very seriously. It should come as no surprise that those managers who couldn't let go of micromanaging, who didn't trust or empower their employees—they consistently scored lower on engagement from quarter to quarter. The irony is these often-new managers could often be seen hanging out with the employees after work every Friday, still part of the team in that sense—but when it came to overseeing that same team, they just couldn't let them do their work without close eyes on them.

It will drive you crazy attempting to chase down the details of what all of your employees are doing or are *supposed* to be doing. You can't do that. That's why you're given rein to hire employees in the first place: your leaders know you can't do that because they don't want to do that either.

Getting to that realization might be at the end of a steep learning curve for you. I've seen that curve be much steeper in engineering organizations than I've ever seen it in a sales, marketing, or service organization. It's deeply tied to that engineering mentality of perfection. During a code review, everybody gets to see your code and knows if you made a mistake, and you don't want to be the person who makes it.

Remember that on an individual level, your stupid mistakes are yours alone. You can own them easily. If you're a leader and you're critical, exacting, and demanding of your team, you are setting unrealistic expectations for everyone, including yourself. It can form not only an unpleasant workplace but a dysfunctional one, which is often far worse.

"LET'S REMEMBER WHY WE'RE HAVING THIS MEETING"

When you get more than two people in a room, it's easy to forget why you're in there in the first place.

Let's say that you and I are going into a meeting to discuss whether or not to change the wrappers on Hershey's Kisses from silver to black for whatever reason. You and I can go into the room, understand that's going to be the discussion, and stay on that topic for thirty minutes or so.

Then a third person comes in. They ask what color the little piece of paper that's attached to the wrapper is going to be. Will that stay white or will it be black too? Is it silver? How are we going to package them now?

Now imagine twenty people in that room. Now people are suggesting that while we change the color of the wrapper, we might as well change the shape while we're at it. No other candies are shaped that way. Let's make them round or flat.

When so many people are involved in a meeting, it's incredibly easy for things to spiral away from the core topic, such that you end up exiting the meeting never making a decision about your intended topic. Instead, you end up with mid-level project managers who want their ideas heard that end up creating a dozen new meetings to discuss a dozen new things that are almost unrelated to the original discussion at hand.

A tactic that has worked well for me in meetings is to use a baton. The only person allowed to speak is the one holding it. Everyone else is required to listen until the baton is handed to the next person for their turn to speak. It keeps meetings focused. It prevents side conversations and outbursts. There is nothing worse for the productivity of a meeting than when three different conversations are occurring at once. It also curbs people speaking just so they can say they spoke because they feel like they have to if they've been invited.

Manage your meetings. Keep your team and others on topic, and keep them short. I don't know where the idea came from that all meetings need to be scheduled for an hour, but knock that off. I'm a huge fan of the fifteen-minute meeting. Granted, if you have more than a five-person team that might not be feasible, but a thirty-minute one certainly is. You know you're in for a bad meeting when there are coffee, cupcakes, and doughnuts laid out. That means you're expected to be there for the duration. #Suckage

Be protective and respectful of your team's time. Don't let them get pulled into meetings where you know their time will be wasted. Many times, your job as a leader will be to attend those meetings in their stead and suffer for them to ensure they don't get pulled off the line and out of their rhythm. It's been said that it takes the average engineer or programmer forty-five minutes to get back into their flow after every interruption. That is an excess of lost productivity. Hence the headphones.

Meetings are another tool that must be used in the right way. If you don't run the meeting, keep your employees away whenever possible. Your team will be better for it. #LetYourTeamsRun

YOU HAVE TO ASK FOR HELP

When it comes to ensuring you have the right tools for the right job, it is crucial that you add asking for help as a tool in your belt.

I've seen so many engineers and tech types move into leadership roles and burn out because while they're great at managing projects, they suck at managing people. What they failed to realize is that there are no projects without people attached. If you're going to manage projects, you're going to have to deal with the human beings involved.

When that burnout occurs, they'll often ask to move back to an individual contributor role. Some of them may be asked to leave because they didn't realize they were failing. The forward-thinking engineers that realize they're failing, though? They're the easiest ones to deal with because they will generally ask someone for help. They will look for internal support from the company to improve their leadership skills. They can handle the honest conversation when a leader tells them that they were always great as an individual contributor, and maybe it is time to return to that role to keep the team strong.

Being able to do that? That's a sign of leadership in and of itself: to recognize that stepping back is better for the team and having the strength of character to do so. When that happened, at least in our company, they would keep the pay bump that accompanied the move into leadership. While it might not make sense to some, if you were valuable as an independent contributor—so much so that you were promoted to management—then you're still worth the money you were paid to move into that position.

Companies can do a much better job of educating engineers as they're transitioning into these roles. They need to let them know not only the expectations but the outs—the best way to exit if they find the position truly isn't for them. These candidates need to be able to tap out after three or six months without the paralyzing fear of losing their job. It's a perfect opportunity to offer them additional management training if they're willing to stick it out or a clean escape if they are not—a safe place to land.

As important as it is to ask for help when you're making the transition, it's equally important for you to ask for help from your employees when you are a leader. I've gone to my employees on more than one occasion to tell them my neck is in the wringer because I overpromised, or I made a miscalculation and the correction is more than I can handle on my own. Trust that they will step up to the task. Everybody likes to be a member of a winning team, the team that could turn it around, whatever "it" is.

Asking your peers for help is crucial to relationship building and important to your success as a future leader. Your peers might have more or less experience than you do in different facets of the business, but one thing they will absolutely have is an alternative perspective from yours as well as a different set of personal experiences that they bring to the table. I don't mean experience they gained by going to this class or a mastery of those certain fundamentals. I mean experiences with different people and different teams.

Building these relationships opens doors to all kinds of possibilities. I've gone to leadership peers and "borrowed" employees from them for certain projects that necessitated their expertise and vice versa. We are invested in each other's success.

As part of this process, companies also need to do a better job of letting these transitioning managers know that they have the ability to fail and not just in a "we don't care if you succeed" fashion. They need to know they will be supported—that the company will work with them, provide them with the tools and the training—but also that it's not the end of the road if it doesn't work out. That the company still values you. You have an allowance to fuck up. An allowance—not a bank account you can withdraw from.

KNOW WHICH TOOLS YOU NEED TO ACQUIRE

Sometimes the best decision you can make as a leader is not to make a decision.

Leaders make not only tactical decisions on a daily basis but strategic ones. Sometimes that strategic decision might be to not make a decision that day. They think, *I'm not going to act on that today. I've got bigger fish in the frying pan, and that problem can wait three months.*

Every day, leaders make strategic decisions such as what software tool their team will be using next year. Take Slack, for example. Normally for tools like Slack, you sign a year contract, and every twelve months they're up for review. Some people love it, some people hate it. Some people simply prefer other chat or group communication tools.

You've got to think six months ahead of time if you're thinking strategically. You make the decision every day when you're interacting with your employees and finding out how they feel about the software. You have to be able to pick the right tool at the right time and the right place.

If it's a tactical decision and all I need to do is hammer a nail in the wall—and I haven't done that in the last year and can't foresee doing it in the next two years—maybe I just go out, buy a hammer, and pound that one nail.

Tactical decision made. However, maybe what I need to invest in is pneumatic air guns that are going to cost the company $150,000 because I can foresee us putting in thousands of nails in the future. That's a different type of decision. I'm not going to go out and buy a thousand hammers when I need a million nails.

Think more strategically about what future problems might be, based on what the current problems are. If you can do that, you're going to have a much better time in management. If you can see around corners, you're going to be a rock star, though most won't know it because you'll be solving problems before they occur.

The challenge is that you engineers and tech geeks tend to focus on the now and near now. Like I have done. You're used to product and coding life cycles. You don't think about the fact that a product needs to be ready in December because another major launch in another department is reliant on it.

It's hard to remember that your task is draining the swamp when you're up to your knees in alligators.

Said another way, it's tough to see that big picture. That's one of the chasms you'll have to cross from being an individual contributor or even a small-team manager into higher leadership positions. You have to be more cognizant of how all the pieces are connected. Everything can break if you don't understand the interdependencies.

This is why relationships with your peers are so important. In the next chapter, I will discuss why forming those allegiances is critical to your success as you move up the food chain.

Remember—everything can work better when you work with others.

CHAPTER SEVEN

BUILDING ALLEGIANCES

As a mid-level manager, you can't be expected to know what's going on in the company every day, but what you should understand is what is going on that involves your team. That means the external things that touch your team, that influence them, and that bind or constrain them, or the opportunities that are presented to your team because of the other dependencies that affect them. You should always at least be aware of that immediate cone that surrounds them.

There is no more effective way of finding all of this out than sitting down with a peer for fifteen minutes over a cup of coffee or meeting at the water cooler or in the smoking area if that's your collective thing. Don't do it at the planned meetings with twenty people, where everybody goes over everything they're working on—the meeting that takes four hours where everyone is brain dead after the first hour. Sure, they might perk up when you're talking about their group, and vice versa, but you're both losing all the context around it.

You get that context by making those individual relationships with your peers. When your peers understand that you're interested in their work—and by extension, interested in them—they feel that you're invested in helping them succeed. As a result, they will reciprocate that. They won't accidentally leave out a key piece of information that you need for your success because you've been helping them win. They want you to win so you can stay there and help them win more.

MANAGEMENT IS A MORAL ACT

gapingvoid
Culture Design Group

@gapingvoid

Allegiances can help prevent your having to fire a valuable member of your team even if they did something colossally stupid. Of course, I have a story about this.

An employee of mine wrote a post on Google Plus. This employee happened to have a couple of million followers on social media; this is to say everything he wrote was extremely well read. He wrote about an HR system that we had been using at the company, and let's just say he wasn't a fan. What we will say is he ripped them a new one in this post. There were hundreds of thousands of comments, mostly from other people who were also using this product, as well their employees, all bitching about the mobile app: how it didn't allow them to scan receipts and other functionality issues.

The employee had written the post late in the evening, so come morning, we walked into a shitstorm. The post was too big to delete; too many people had seen it and commented on it. Honestly, the worst thing we could have done would have been to delete it because as the saying goes, "Once tweeted, never deleted." People take screenshots. There are caches. There's the Internet Archive's Wayback Machine. Nothing goes away.

The company was obviously outraged, and I got the order from on high to fire the employee. I told them that they'd have to fire me just to hire someone to fire him, and that deleting the post would be the worst decision they could make. Once we were able to agree that we wouldn't fire him outright, they next told me I had to have him write an apology post to the HR company. That wasn't happening either.

Here's where allegiances come in.

I first went to a number of my leadership peers and told them the story. Once I had their agreement, we teamed up and went back to senior leadership. We admitted that the post was embarrassing to both us and the customer. It was still the truth. The software sucked. Secondly, we were all in agreement that the employee was an idiot for posting it. However, he had no idea that the company was our provider as well as our customer. He honestly had no way of knowing that.

What we did come up with was a compromise. We sent the employee to the company where he met with the CEO and CMO. He did an interview with them, part of which was for public consumption. He spent over half a day there, part of which entailed him walking their leadership through the facets of their software that were burdensome to work with, particularly for him. He traveled twenty days a month. His expense reports every month were thirty to forty pages long. That meant scanning every receipt and loading it into their system so it could then be viewed as a PDF. It was archaic. I would have had to hire at least one full-time administrative assistant to manage that workload.

The thing is that the company had never seen anybody with that kind of workload try to use their system. Once they saw it, they had a moment of clarity and agreed with almost everything he had to say.

The company came back to our leadership and said, "Look, we understand it now. The guy's got a point." They agreed to work with us, and specifically the employee, to try and fix the problem. They watched his workflow more carefully to find ways to lessen the burden. In the end, they drastically refined their software and process to accommodate workloads of that size. The change increased the value of the company many times over, and they're now a publicly traded company.

None of that would have happened had I not built allegiances with leadership peers and above beforehand.

I had to know the right people to reach out to so they would join my cause. I had to understand their concerns and know that they would be looking at this with the same perspective as me. Had I not known those peers, I could have never called them and asked them to risk their neck by arguing against senior leadership. I didn't have to explain why it affected them because they already knew from our previously established lines of mutual communication and respect. There was no hard sell. I knew immediately who the right people were to call.

Believe me, there were other people I could have called who would have been vehemently opposed to my agenda. We publicly bad-mouthed a customer. While the employee never identified them as such because he didn't know, people commenting identified who the company was and that they were in fact our customer; that's where things got dicey.

Marketing didn't want to see the post taken down, as they knew our competitors would use that against us. PR certainly didn't want the resultant shitstorm of forcing an employee to remove an honest post. HR didn't want to deal with the fallout of firing an employee for speaking his mind on a personal social media account. All of those people combined had a much larger voice and a more compelling voice than mine alone, and thanks to the allegiances I'd already formed within those divisions, we were able to get senior leadership to see things our way.

MAKE FRIENDS EARLY

Before you make the transition to management, it's smart to start forming relationships, not just with those who may become your leadership peers, but with those on your team who might also have the potential to be your boss at some point. The best way you can do that is to be helpful to your coworkers. Volunteer your help when they need it, even in times when you're busy and don't want to, especially if you know you're the right person to help with that job at that time.

Understand the workloads of your coworkers. Whether we're discussing coders or factory workers, their workloads are cyclical. There is a Toyota plant in San Antonio, and I've got friends who work there. Toward the beginning of the summer, they start slowing down their line because it's time for the end of their production run for that model year. They're preparing to ramp up, knowing that come the fall when the new line is reduced again, the Tundras will be flying down the line again.

The same happens in coding and engineering. One month it might be my time that's getting hammered with work, but in the next month, we might have delivered on our product, making that next month easy. Meanwhile, in that same month, my coworker or peer might be getting slammed. That's the time to build coalitions by stepping up to help them, even when you don't have to. You do it because you know you're going to need their help in the future.

It might be hard for you as an engineer or tech geek to

grasp this concept because you often work in isolation. It's a challenge for you to build these coalitions even within your own team. Most of your socialization with your coworkers likely occurs after you've all met your quota at work and you meet somewhere quiet, enjoying cold beverages and talking because none of you engage in an excess of conversation during your normal working day.

It is therefore harder for you to build these early allegiances. When you find yourself in management, it's often a surprise. You weren't looking for it, nor were you expecting it. Maybe your manager was promoted and recommended you for a bump as well. Maybe your manager got fired and your exemplary work made you a natural fit for his replacement. Whatever the case, you find yourself surprised and unprepared.

Prepare now. Build those relationships.

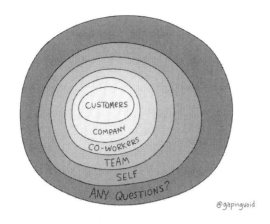

CUSTOMERS
COMPANY
CO-WORKERS
TEAM
SELF
ANY QUESTIONS?

gapingvoid
Culture Design Group

@gapingvoid

F.U.D.

I once had a phenomenal boss who took three months of leave after having her first child. Two days before she was due to return to work, she decided that she wanted to stay home and raise her baby. Her husband made enough money, and she was in love with being a mother. The next day, I found myself in a meeting with the chairman of the company, who was now running corporate communications due to my boss's unexpected departure.

There were six of us in the room. He told us he needed a new leader. Nobody raised their hand, including me. I was brand new to the group, having been in the division for less than a week. I hardly knew the other people in the room. Then the chairman pointed to me and said, "Rob, you're the most seasoned guy here. I want you to be the interim leader."

That's when I was hit with F.U.D.—fear, uncertainty, and doubt—the same three things you'll undoubtedly encounter as an engineer thrust into a leadership role.

There was a woman on that team in charge of corporate governance. I didn't know anything about corporate governance, our company giving, or our charitable organizations; I didn't really know what they did. I didn't know how they got funded. I knew I had a payroll deduction that went toward it. That was the extent of my knowledge.

This is to say that while I had already held some leadership positions with other companies in different capacities, I was thrown into this with so much to learn. All of sudden, I became this team's boss, interim or not. I knew some of them resented it, even though they didn't raise their hands. In fact, I learned later that some of them wanted the role but wanted to talk to the chairman in private.

That left me having to patch relationships right from the get-go. Fortunately, I was able to find a replacement for the position permanently, and in doing so, I improved my relationships with the rest of the team because the candidate was someone they all loved. This paved the way for future allegiances should I have ever needed their assistance in the future.

MAKING TRADES

While I was in corporate communications, I often knew about things like employee layoffs before they happened because I had to be briefed. I had to be in the know if we were going to lose a board member or if a senior vice president was leaving the company.

On more than one occasion, if I became aware that a "reduction in force" layoff was coming, I'd go to my boss and ask him directly if my team was going to be affected. When he told me, "No," I used the opportunity to tell him that there were some members who *should* be affected for the betterment of the team. It was a chance to upgrade some of the skillsets in my department and increase productivity, costing the company less money in the long run.

I've also made department trades with teams that cross my department, such as graphic design. I relied on them heavily for marketing and advertising materials, and they were always backed up with requests from other departments. If I had someone on my team who wasn't a great performer in my division and maybe not the best fit, I'd arrange a trade with design to see if they could be of help and in better alignment there. It ended up being helpful to me and the team twofold.

Don't only think of head counts on your team in terms of the people that report to you, and certainly don't relate them only to reductions. Consider them when your company is doing well and hiring like crazy. There was a point at Rackspace when we were hiring 120 people a month. We were growing so quickly that we couldn't hire recruiters fast enough to fill all of the open positions.

MANAGEMENT DOESN'T HURT.

GROWING HURTS.

gapingvoid
Culture Design Group

@gapingvoid

Managing growth is just as important as managing reductions. The last thing you want to do is overgrow your department. When times are good, it's easy to add people, but in six months to a year, when business hits its slow cycle, you don't want to let go three people you hired just twelve months ago. You think you struggle to manage people when things are going fine? Imagine when you're faced with *that* conversation.

Beyond the uncomfortable discussion that accompanies such a decision, there is the cost to consider. Firing someone shortly after hiring them, as we've covered previously, is quite expensive. On average, an engineer needs to work for a company for eighteen to twenty-four months for the company to get back their initial cost from the hire. Engineer salaries are high. They often expect benefits like stock options, grants, and equity. Even on a four-year vesting period, that's very expensive to unravel.

For example, say you give an employee $100,000 worth of stock at 25 percent every year. If the employee leaves at the end of that year, either due to downsizing or unhappiness, they keep 25 percent of that stock. The other 75 percent of it has already been allocated to them, even though they're not with the company anymore. That means no one else in the company can use it to entice new hires. It's locked up until the vesting period is over.

The only way the company can free that stock is by going back to the board for a stock option buyback, which is very complex and involves the Securities Exchange Commission and a number of other legal issues. Most companies prefer to wait it out until they can put the stocks back into the pool. That is a huge expense to have that equity inaccessible for so long when they could be putting it to more productive use.

This says nothing of the cost involved in relocating and training these engineers to get them up to speed on your code. If you've hired them from a car company and they're now working for a hosting company, while they're still coding in the same language, it's for an altogether different beast.

Managing growth both upward and downward is absolutely critical, but most people are horrible at it in both directions. Foster your relationships across departments and look for opportunities where you can be helpful. In the case of graphic design, if I help them hire another designer, I'm going to regain productivity for my programmers. That amounts to more money, happy employees, and happy customers. Product is shipped faster, and bugs are fixed more quickly. Sales is ecstatic because they can sell products earlier in the cycle. Leadership is happy because the stock is doing better. Everyone wins.

Don't just make trades with your people. For five years, I had a cartoonist on retainer. He worked for almost every department in the company. He designed banner ads, T-shirts for events, and artwork for our customer welcome center. His work was phenomenal, and as such, didn't come cheap.

Knowing that, all of the work he did for the other departments was billed to mine. He was already doing more work for me than he was for them. However, when we went into budget meetings my last year with the company, there was another department that I knew needed more money. In the current environment—having been recently purchased by a private equity firm looking to cut costs anywhere they could—I knew there was little chance they'd see how the cartoonist's work was helping to build our internal culture and customer relations. It was only a matter of time before they killed it. I cut it out of my budget and transferred the money to the department in need.

That's building coalitions.

WE'RE ALMOST THERE

If you've stuck with my droning on this long, then you deserve a word of congratulations.

Stick with me for one more chapter. Whereas before we talked about how to talk to senior leadership, now we're going in the other direction to give you advice on how to shut the fuck up and listen.

CHAPTER EIGHT

LISTEN MORE THAN YOU TALK

We managed to piss off the CEO of a major US airline, and he wasn't afraid to tell me *all* about it.

He had good cause to be irate. We were in the post-9/11 sphere of air travel and as a result of an issue on our end, his ticketing system went down. The ticketing system being down means his airline is down. If his planes can't get off the ground, there is a domino effect. The way the industry works, if one plane is twenty minutes late, the next plane is going to be an hour late, and the one following is going to be two hours late. It creates a veritable shitstorm, and it is almost impossible to catch up. It's hard enough just to stay on time on a routine basis.

Someone on this CEO's team found my personal phone

number on my Twitter account. I was responding to other customers at the time, and while I was using my personal Twitter handle, I always used the Rackspace hashtag so that it would be captured by our internal tools. That also allowed for my team to see it and follow the conversation.

The next thing I know, I'm speaking with the airline CEO, and he is nothing short of livid. When I say that he was screaming and cussing, I'm not speaking in hyperbole. He was, quite literally, yelling and swearing at me. When it was clear he wasn't going to stop, I knew nothing productive was going to occur as long as I let him continue in that vein.

I told him to shut the fuck up. Not politely, either. I screamed back at him and said, "Right now, I'm the guy that's going to help you."

There was an audible sigh on the line. It might have been because he anticipated my asking if he'd unplugged the power to his cable modem for thirty seconds before plugging it back in to reboot the ticketing system. However, it was likely a sigh of relief because afterward, he was calm. He listened. I was able to tell him that our team was already in contact with his engineers working on the problem, which was true.

While he let loose his initial tirade, I was in our internal chat room where I observed that my team had already connected with the engineers that managed the servers for this particular airline. In fact, we had already resolved the issue, but we hadn't informed the customer because we wanted to verify it for certain. I was, however, able to inform the CEO that by the time he had calmed down that we had already fixed his problem, his engineers would be notified shortly, and that they would be able to process tickets at that moment.

SCARY CHANGE IS WHEN YOU GROW THE MOST.

gapingvoid
Culture Design Group

@gapingvoid

I KNOW WHAT YOU'RE THINKING

Remember how I told you that I want you to learn just as much from my mistakes as from my successes?

This would be one of those instances. The exception here is that this particular story contains examples of what you should *and* shouldn't do.

Let me be clear: it is *never* acceptable for someone to be verbally berated by a customer, whether they are a staff person or the head of the company. Having said that, I am not advocating that you tell high-ranking executive customers to shut the fuck up, at least not as a standing rule. At least not on your work phone, where those calls can be recorded. You didn't hear that from me.

In all seriousness, there *is* a viable lesson here.

I'm not ashamed to say I'm a Judge Judy fan, and she uses a phrase I love: "God gave you two ears and one mouth for a reason." He wants you to listen twice as often as you speak. Was it right for the CEO to lay into me the way he had? Certainly not. Did he need to do it for me to be able to give him the resolution he needed? Certainly not. But I understood his perspective—he wanted some fucking attention and he fucking wanted it right fucking now.

While it might feel foreign to you as an engineer or tech geek, it is of critical importance to recognize when a customer, whether internal or external, needs to vent. In this case, the airline CEO realized he was under stress and acting inappropriately. On a subsequent call, he apologized to me. Not only that, we ended up forming a friendship where we would talk at least once a month, up until he left that role.

Though my response was not exactly the right one, I did listen to what he had to say. I let him vent until it no longer became appropriate, and listening like that was a lesson that served me well.

When I would get a text message from our CEO that only had a phone number and no other message, I knew there was a pissed customer, and that I needed to call. I'd look up the number in the system to find out exactly who they were, but I wouldn't look at any other metric. I didn't want to know how much money they were spending. I didn't want to know how high profile they were. I only wanted a name. If they called or emailed our CEO directly, there was a good chance I'd be speaking to someone at a high level in the customer's company.

On one such occasion, I ended up speaking with the original CEO of the Scooter Store, a multimillion-dollar mobility-scooter chain. I didn't want to know what they were spending with us because I didn't want my perception of them to be altered by that. It didn't matter to me if someone was spending $14 a month or $14 million a year on our service. I wanted to solve their problem.

I was forced to listen because I didn't read the complaint tickets. I didn't see the history, and I didn't want to hear what the customer's issues were from the tech's perspective. I always wanted to hear it from the customer first.

Only then would I go back to read the tickets and talk to our engineers to discover where the disconnect was because in truth, there always is one—either someone didn't hear someone or they didn't hear something correctly—communication can't happen effectively if two people are talking at the same time.

Listening is the most effective way for you to gather information. It is also an extremely effective way of calming down an irate customer, as long as they're not speaking down to you or demeaning you or your team in any way. When you listen, when you actually let them talk, that anger almost always dissipates. It doesn't go away, but it allows them to get to a point where they feel heard and you can work together on a solution.

It's not enough to understand the technical aspects of their problem. You must understand what the problem actually means to the customer. In the case of the airline, it's a serious problem for them not to be able to board passengers because it means they can't fly. They can't make it to a particular destination, which means the people in that destination can't board that flight to, in turn, get where *they* were going.

The engineers only concern themselves with the technical aspect of the problem and relying on them for all of my information removes information vital to my solving the customer's issue. Empathy and situation have to come into play, not just numbers, data, and hard facts. This can be particularly challenging when you have an engineer on your end speaking to an engineer on the customer side. There can be a clash of egos and finger-pointing.

That's where you come in. It's your job to get them focused on solving the problem at hand and not determining who is at fault. Forensics can and will always be performed after the fact. A root-cause analysis must be done to ensure that the same mistake doesn't occur twice.

When you assume a position where the buck stops with you in terms of customer satisfaction, open your ears and close your mouth.

LISTEN TO YOUR INTERNAL CUSTOMERS

Engineers sometimes get painted with too wide a brush, even unfairly at times. Because I am one of you, however, this is not one of those times.

The profile of an engineer is generally that of an introvert. Extroverts don't generally pursue a profession that ties them to a keyboard, staring at a monitor for fifteen hours a day. Engineers hide from their bosses. They hide from their coworkers. They hide from just about everyone.

If you're going to remain an individual contributor, then you can continue to do that without a problem. If you're reading this book, however, that's not your plan. If you're going to listen to your customers, either internal or external, you're going to have to step into the daylight and stop hiding.

Every time we identified a Twitter handle as being a Racker, we would flag them. From that point on, everything they tweeted was in our system, for better or for worse. More often than not, it was for the better. We'd often find someone who submitted something to an open-source project that they were devoted to—one that would help the entire programming community, not just Rackspace.

When we located them, we would talk to those people and put them in our social media ambassadors course, which gave them extra training to use their social media feeds to become more vocal and to speak within their realm of expertise on behalf of the company. Some of them turned into superstars within their own community, whether it be coding or any other group. They were invited to speaking gigs and became almost minicelebrities. At work, they became far more outgoing.

The true introvert with the earbuds in, staring at the monitor all day long? There's a good chance they don't have a social media feed. They're not the type of engineer who maintains a blog. Your chances of turning them into a terrific listener are greatly reduced. In cases like those, you must surround them with people who are good listeners.

One way we solved this was to have account managers, some of whom had been engineers in a past life, on calls where our engineers had to speak to the customer's engineers. Their job was, in essence, to translate the customer's pain. They helped to ease the burden on the engineers, especially in the cases of "bad news" calls. Engineers hate bad news. They're firemen without helmets. They want to be thought of as the ones who rush into the burning building to put out the blaze, except with code. They fix bugs and get a customer's infrastructure back online remarkably quickly, and that's where they get their adrenaline rush.

Because of this, they shy away from "bad news" situations. Staying away from them means they don't get experience with them, so they never become adept at handling them. This perpetuates them avoiding them even more. They then never learn how to handle that bad news—to listen to their customers to find the best way to resolve their problems.

The only way to learn to listen, particularly to upset customers, is through repetition. You will learn—at a rate that surprises you—what truly motivates a person's anger. Sometimes you'll discover that they're legitimately pissed at you and your team for dropping the ball. Other times they're actually angry at themselves because they missed some detail but want to redirect that anger at you. Others still are just legitimate asshats, and those are the ones you want to fire and send to your competitor because they're simply not worth your bandwidth.

In order to fully develop your ability to listen to your customers, you're going to have to rip off the bandage and put yourself in uncomfortable situations. Lean on others to help you manage the anxiety and fear until you can stand on your own. Get experience by doing calls with people who have done it before to learn the nuances of when to speak and when to be quiet; when to agree, even when the customer might be wrong; and when to disagree.

Whatever you do, don't hide. Developing this listening skill is critical to your future as a leader.

THE RIGHT THING ISN'T ALWAYS THE RIGHT THING

We once had a customer all over us on social media for three days straight, complaining that Rackspace was overbilling him. He said that he had discontinued our service three months ago but was still receiving statements. We reached out to him via our social accounts and asked him to email or call us, but he never responded.

We were finally able to track him down. It turned out he *had* shut down his main account, but he hadn't deleted all of his data from our storage repository and was being billed $1.17 a month for the three months he mentioned. I called him and asked him for his PayPal account identifier. I told him I'd pay *him* what he owed *us*, plus ten additional dollars for his inconvenience if he would stop bad-mouthing us.

His attitude totally changed. He went so far as to apologize on social media and shared that we paid him the money and that he was in the wrong in the first place.

His account manager wasn't exactly pleased with me because in truth the customer *did* owe us the money, but what is a reputation worth? It's certainly worth a hell of a lot more than ten dollars. Paying to make the problem go away in some instances makes longer-term financial sense for your company.

If you're on a team that gets paid a bonus based on MRR—monthly recurring revenue—anything that reduces that MRR can affect your bonus, and you certainly don't want that. However, if you're only looking at it through that lens, similar to engineers only looking at code and facts, you're missing other important information. What if this same complaining customer is also taking up 35 percent more of our support time than other customers who are paying similar amounts? Where's our gross margin then? Where's our profit? Those factors considered, gross margin essentially doesn't exist.

Maybe paying them to go away isn't the best thing for you or your team or even the company in the short term; public companies have to report their earnings every quarter. However, you as a leader have to balance the best thing over time for everyone involved. Even if you can't make everyone happy, your goal is to make as many people happier as possible.

In essence, you have to listen to the problem and consider all the angles to come up with the best *long-term* solution.

YOU'RE UP FOR REVIEW

As a manager, in addition to being responsible for providing reviews to your employees, you'll also be subject to their review.

A sure sign you're doing something wrong in how you communicate with your employees is if you're surprised by anything an employee has to say about your performance. It's an indication that you're not listening. If you're communicating with your employees—listening as much if not more than you talk—nothing should come from left field.

You might also be subject to reviews by your peers. In truth, it's harder to anticipate surprises there. It's not likely you'll speak with them as often. They're off running their portion of the business while you're busy managing yours. Someplace in the middle, the parts of those businesses touch, and when they do, it can be like tectonic plates rubbing together.

We know what happens when that occurs.

Different leadership peers have different styles as well as different goals within the company. Everyone wants to make big money with sizable bonus checks, but your method of getting there might be more strategic while your peers are more tactical. You focus on the big picture and the long game while they're centered on the next month or three, and so they don't understand your plans, nor do you understand theirs.

Once you have enough of these peer reviews under your belt and you've been surprised enough times, it should dawn on you that it is as important to get to know those peers as well as you know your own employees. That's not an easy feat when you're both managers. It's not easy to find fifteen minutes for coffee or even just a brief chat in the hallway.

Make the effort. Try for dinner once a month. Settle for five minutes of water cooler chat instead of fifteen. You'll see those surprises diminish rather quickly.

Let's be honest, part of that has to do with the fact that when people know someone and begin to build a relationship with them, they're much less likely to say negative things about the other person. If they do, you now have an avenue to address it with them one-on-one. It gives you an opportunity to truly listen to their feedback so that you both can move forward in improving your working relationship, which of course is better for your respective teams and the company as a whole.

Listening more than you talk is also crucial when giving your employees recommendations and reviews. When someone asks me for a job recommendation, I tell them to write it and then give it to me. If I agree with it, I'll sign it. If I don't, I won't. The thing is they only get one shot at it because it forces them to be honest. They'll take ownership of failure. They'll tell me the things they think I see in them. It gives me a chance to listen to what they believe I think of them, which is invaluable information.

This is a terrific practice in reviews as well. Before I'd give them the results, I'd ask them: "How do you personally think you're doing? What do you think are your coworkers' opinions of you?"

Generally, they were quite confident in what they thought of themselves and the perception of their work, but rarely did they have a high level of confidence in what their peers thought of them. This opened the door for me to coach them to talk more with their coworkers. Build relationships with them. Listen to them. One day they could be your boss, or you could be theirs. It's important to know how the other ticks.

Sound familiar?

Listening to what employees think of themselves gives you excellent insight into their insecurities and what motivates them. Imposter syndrome can take the legs out of the best employee, and it can reveal itself in reviews conducted this way. It provides you with the opportunity to give them that critical reinforcement that they're vital to the team and to continue with the excellent work they produce.

Many times, their fears, uncertainties, and doubts can shed light on areas that need improvement that you might not have seen:

"I'm afraid I'm being asked to do too much."

"I don't think what I'm being asked to do makes sense."

"I have doubts about the company in the long term."

Instead of scheduling a ten-minute meeting where you simply give them their score based on whatever ranking system HR has put together, take the time, however much it entails, to truly listen to what they think and hear what they feel. You'll be amazed at what you learn.

THE END OF THE ROAD

I've said a lot of shit, some of it harsh, and most of it true.

The harshness comes from a need to be honest with my fellow tech geeks and engineers because you are my people. It's my contention that when it comes to leadership, you've been done a disservice because people don't know what to do with your unique and unusual talents.

Follow me for a few more pages to what I promise is a logical conclusion to my nonsensical ramblings.

CONCLUSION

IT'S NOT YOUR FAULT

Look, I know it doesn't seem like I'm telling you anything revolutionary here.

You're right.

The thing is, you need to hear this from me because you're just naturally so bad at it.

You're built to think a certain way, and it's not a bad one. It's just different. If engineers actually do want to join a conversation—and we know that's a rarity—they want to own the conversation.

We had an email list called San Antonio Fun. It was an email group on Outlook where you could talk about basically anything. You could sell stuff or just engage in random chitchat. About ten years ago, someone asked the question: if you built a giant treadmill and put an airplane on it, could the airplane take off because the runway, the treadmill, was moving?

On this thread of engineers, there were a fuckton of emails arguing about whether or not a plane could take off from a theoretical, nonexistent treadmill. Of course, no one was listening to anyone else; they were just "talking" over each other. It wasn't until about five years ago when the show *Myth Busters* answered the question and killed the thread. Prior to that, the thread had been going on for *eight years*.

Engineers like the argument. In their minds, they're not looking for a resolution; they're looking to be right. That doesn't work on the job. They have to find resolutions there, but they can do it with a computer. Most times they don't have to reason with a human being to fix the problem; they just fix it.

Companies bear some blame in cultivating the negatives of these behaviors. They let them put in their earbuds. They let them sit in the dark. They let them close themselves off and sit in front of their computers, whether in a cubicle or an office. They "raise" them to be as they are. Then all of a sudden, they open the door, turn on the lights, and say, "Tomorrow you're going to be a manager!" and then wonder why they fail.

The goal of this book is to try to give you the tools to reframe your skills and your mindset. We don't want to *change* your skills. We want to change how you think about them.

Learn to trust and rely on the people who yesterday were your peers. As a new manager, you have trouble relying on your employees because you're used to being the fireman that climbs the ladder to enter the burning building alone. You had control of your destiny to become the hero. You now have to see yourself as the fire chief. You can't go in the burning building now because if we lose you, we lose the man in control.

Own your mistakes, as contradictory as it might be to

your internal programming. You're outside of the bubble now. Now is not the time to perform like an individual contributor where you can hunt down a bad piece of code you might have written and fix it before anyone notices. Trust your team enough to be transparent when you've done wrong. It will inspire confidence in you and lead to greater cohesiveness.

Be helpful. The number one role of a leader is to help their employees. It's not to win or to make your sales goal. If your employees aren't winning, then you won't either. Remember: if you don't win, someone else is going to lose as a result.

You're a perfectionist. Recognize, though, that the pursuit of perfection is almost always going to be to the detriment of the company. You can't be perfect. What you can be is good enough and better than most. In doing so, you'll be bigger than most. We all want to have 100 percent customer satisfaction and guaranteed uptime, but those are cheerleading metrics. Accept and understand that you're allowed to fail the right way, in the right places, at the right time. Be right 80 percent of the time when it counts, and be wrong when it doesn't.

We've established that you're probably not good at conversation. If you're not good at conversation, then you can't be good at confrontation. You want to please, and so you avoid confrontation. As a manager, your senior leaders trust you to tell them when their baby is ugly. Even if you're wrong, as long as you do it in a respectful manner, or if you come with an alternative plan of action, your bosses will return that respect. They'll know they made the right decision by putting you in a position of increased responsibility.

Replace yourself. Your employees want meaningful work. They want opportunities. They want to feel needed. They want a path to grow. As a leader, you have to provide that for them. Train your employees to do your job so that you can move them into it, allowing you to move into a job that hopefully someone else is preparing *you* for.

You want a drill or a hole? Know which problem you're solving. Otherwise you're going to be *wrong* 80 percent of the time. It's that simple.

Build those allegiances. Your employees are either going to push you up the ladder or push you out the door. Your peers will promote your voice or stifle it. If you help them, they will feel compelled to help you back. It's a damn simple idea, but when communication isn't a strength, simple can feel quite complicated.

Simplest of all, open those ears, close your mouth, and listen. Everyone has something to teach you, and as a leader, you'd better be surrounding yourself with people smarter than you so you always have something to learn.

WHAT'S NEXT

Like a choose-your-own-adventure, now that you've reached this point, go back to the beginning. Read the book again. I'll wait.

Start talking to others who have recently become new managers. Find out how they're doing with their transition and see what resources the company made available to them for their new role. Find out what roadblocks they've run into and how they overcame them, if at all. If they've struggled, give them my book. Reach out to me on Facebook and tell me your story. I want to hear from you.

Above all, embrace the newness of this role. You were once a caterpillar in your cubicle chrysalis, and now you've broken out.

You're going to be able to fly.

Won't that be awesome?

HELP! I'M AN
ENGINEER
STUCK IN A
MANAGER'S
BODY !!!!

ACKNOWLEDGMENTS

It took a large number of people to guide me in life. Here I am thanking just a few of them that were very special to me. I can't thank any of them enough. I'll just list their names—they know who they are.

- Bruce Hughes
- Lew Moorman
- Graham Weston
- Dan Goodgame
- Dave Kroll

And then there are my employees—again, too many to mention. I collectively leave them a huge thank you.

Finally, to my friend Rocky. We lost you too soon.

Rob

ABOUT THE AUTHOR

One of six brothers, Rob grew up in a small farming community in Illinois. While he was in high school, the family moved to Corpus Christi, Texas, where Rob found an interest in the Navy. After graduating high school, Rob joined the Navy as a medic and worked both as a combat medic and a neonatal respiratory therapist. A lifelong reader, Rob taught himself programming and moved to the tech world in time to help develop Wi-Fi.

While a single parent raising his two children, Rob joined the internet hosting company Rackspace, where he eventually became the vice president of global social strategy. Rob has spent a lifetime reinventing himself and now, in semiretirement, is in the midst of doing so again.